The Japanese in the Monterey Bay Region

THE JAPANESE IN THE
MONTEREY BAY REGION

A BRIEF HISTORY

SANDY LYDON

CAPITOLA BOOK COMPANY

Capitola Book Company
1601 41st Avenue, Capitola, CA 95010

Cover Photo: Mr. and Mrs. G. Wada in the San Juan Valley, c. 1935. Credit: TONI FONTES

Crossed Flag Design, title page: Company logo of the Ide Company of Monterey. It is a detail of a ceremonial jacket celebrating the success of the company in the early 1900s. The jacket is in the collection of the Awa Prefectural Museum, Tateyama City, Chiba Prefecture, Japan.

Library of Congress Cataloging-in-Publication Data

Lydon, Sandy.
    The Japanese in the Monterey Bay Region: A Brief History /
    Sandy Lydon.

        p.   cm.
    ISBN 0-932319-05-X
    Includes bibliographical references and index.
    1. Japanese Americans—California—Monterey Bay Region (Santa Cruz
County, Monterey County, San Benito County)—History. 2. Japanese
Americans—California——Agriculture—History. 3. Japanese
Americans—California—Fishing Industry—History. 4. Japanese
Americans—Evacuation and Relocation, 1942-1945. 5. Japanese
Americans—World War, 1939-1945. 6. Japanese
Americans—California—History—20th century. 7. Monterey Bay Region
(California)—History. I. Title.
979.4'—dc20   94-012045
                                                                      CIP

Contents

PREFACE

This book is a work in progress. It is a template for further research and writing on the history of the Japanese immigrants and their descendants in the Monterey Bay Region. This book is not meant to be the final word on the subject. A much larger work is currently being developed, and the material found here should be seen as the first word on the subject. Certainly not the last.

This book should be viewed as the ruminations of a historian at work. A warm-up. I am testing some theories, ideas, and approaches to see if they work. Some subjects, such as the issue of violence and crime in the Issei community, are being broached for the first time. Others, such as the extent of property transfers from Japanese to non-Japanese during World War II, await further research.

This book is also an exercise to find out what areas are weak. What DON'T we know?

Perhaps the most startling discovery during the preparation of this work was finding out just how front-end-heavy the research and writing on the Japanese has been. Though the story of the Japanese in the region is a century long, the material on the second fifty years is extremely sketchy. The length of Chapter 7, relative to the rest of the book, is a good example of the work that needs to be completed to give the second half of the story some balance.

Suggestions, comments, complaints, questions, and insights are welcome. Please do not hesitate to contact me about anything you see here.

Sandy Lydon
Department of History
Cabrillo College
6500 Soquel Drive
Aptos, CA 95003
Telephone: 408-479-6223
Fax: 408-688-2374
E-Mail: salydon@aol.com

ACKNOWLEDGMENTS

As described later in this book, the concept of *on,* or obligation, is very important in Japanese culture. Throughout the research, writing, and production of this book, I have come to understand the power of the concept. Many people inside and outside of the Japanese community gave of their time and themselves to help move this project forward, and I feel an enormous obligation to them all.

In the beginning it was Yoko and Ben Umeda of Watsonville, the late Seizo Kodani of Point Lobos, the late John Kurasaki and Kay Kamimoto of San Juan, and the late John Gota of Monterey who gave this project its start. Then, in the middle stages, I was assisted by Roy Hattori, Kay Izumizaki, the entire Kodani family, lead by that Sansei whirlwind, Marilyn Kodani, Roy Sakae, Harry Sakesagawa, Mas Hashimoto, and the Reverend Shinryo Sawada.

A number of colleagues and friends reviewed the manuscript, including Tom Takano, Kim Sakamoto, and Rob Edwards. Several classes of students in my Asian American History classes at Cabrillo College used the draft and offered important suggestions. The Cabrillo College administration and Board of Trustees were very generous in their support of this work.

The staffs of the region's county recorders and assessors offices have all been extremely helpful, and a special thanks to John Hodges, County Clerk of San Benito County, for allow-ing us to review the county records as they were being moved from the courthouse to the Wapple House in Hollister. Dick Hill of the San Benito County Historical Society also gave us valuable assistance in that move.

The Santa Cruz County historical community continues to pass along valuable historical leads, and my thanks to Stan Stevens and Phil Reader for thinking of me as they do their own projects. Joanne Resetar, Bill Tao, and Jane Borg shared their valuable work on the 1992 Pajaro Valley Arts Council exhibit, "Nihon Bunka," and Nikki Silva gave me access to all her research on the Japanese in the Pajaro Valley.

Tim Thomas of the Monterey Maritime Museum provided an early preview of the won-drous J.B. Philipps photographs and continues to share photographs and information about the Japanese fishermen. Pat Hathaway, one of the region's true treasures, always has time to work through his mammoth photo archives no matter what else might be pressing him, and Tom Fordham was always there to provide technical advice on the boats and how they worked.

In Tateyama City, Japan, my partner and go-between Kaori Mizoguchi arranged meet-ings and contacts which would have been impossible otherwise. David Green of Hakkakuso provided a place to stay while in Japan. Yoshitomo Fukasawa and Yoshio Ota of the Awa Prefectural Museum provided access to their collection, and Toshio Oba and Masaaki Yamaguchi shared their research on abalone diving on the Boso Peninsula. Bethany Grenald's recent work on the woman divers along the Chiba coast gave me new insights into the problems of diving in cold water. Akiko Shimada Taylor and Ryoko Winter helped translate many of the highly technical documents from Japanese into English. Carolyn Swift and Jo Aribas went into the various county and city offices and plowed through tons of leases, deeds, census reports, and photographs. Jo then took on the responsibility of coordinating the production of this book, a task made doubly difficult by my absence from the country at a crucial stage. Thanks to Judy Steen for her sharp-eyed (and diplomatic) editing. I am grateful (and proud) of my son, Chris, for designing and laying out the book. Mark Ong advised us on some of the design elements, but, in the dark of night, it was Chris who put this book to bed.

A special thanks to Kurt Loesch, my co-author and partner on the Point Lobos project, for allowing this book to butt into the production schedule ahead of our Point Lobos book. Kurt's prowesses at research and persuasion are unmatched, as the sections on abalone diving will attest.

Lillian McPherson Rouse has been extremely generous in her support of our other research and publication projects, and there has been considerable "carry-over" from one project to the other over the years. Regional base maps, for example, were originally done with her support, and many of the photographs were scanned onto CD with her assistance. Lillian's loving hand is behind a lot of what we do.

To my wife Annie goes a special thanks for continuing to gently remind me of the special importance of the Japanese community and supporting the work no matter how long it might take.

Finally, none of this would have happened without the support of George Ow, Jr. His unfailing and unquestioning help on this book, the forthcoming Point Lobos book, the later Japanese book, and the continuing research in the cultural history of the Monterey Bay Region, has been critical. Our collaboration began in the early 1980s with "Chinese Gold," and, over the intervening years, George's patience in all of these projects has been, literally, pure gold.

INTRODUCTION

Though the population of Japanese and their descendants has never exceeded 5% of the region's total population (the high was 4.6% in 1930), they have influenced and enriched the Monterey Bay area beyond their numbers.

At first glance, the story of the Japanese in Monterey, Santa Cruz, and San Benito Counties appears relatively straightforward. Encompassing just over a century from the first recorded arrival of Japanese immigrants, the story builds to an obvious climax with the removal of the community during World War II and then seems to slide smoothly into a happily-ever-after ending.

Upon closer examination, however, the story is not that simple. Fundamental differences between the larger communities of Monterey, Salinas, Watsonville, San Juan Bautista, and Santa Cruz are compounded by the diversity of the Japanese immigrant community. Immigrants ranged from university graduates to the poorest of fishermen and farmers, from prostitutes to the descendants of samurai warriors. Concentration camp experiences were varied as were the experiences of those returning to the regional communities after the war. Finally, immigration from Japan after World War II brought a new group into the region, making the Japanese community even more complex.

INSIDE AND OUTSIDE STORIES

With European immigrants, one can usually give a brief historical and cultural background and then focus on an analysis of the group here in California. However, the saga of the Japanese in the region—the inside story—is complicated by the need to know the national and international context. It is not that the Japanese maintained any closer ties to their homeland than other immigrant groups. Rather it was that non-Japanese would not allow them to break that connection. In the early years a paternalistic Japanese government controlled them, and then, just when the Nisei were getting on their feet and prying the hands of the Japanese government off their affairs, the U.S. government (and non-Japanese population generally) confused them for the pilots flying the airplanes over Pearl Harbor and locked them up in a concentration camp in the Arizona desert. Even today, Japanese Americans in the region are sometimes stalked by the actions of a modern Japanese government and economy, which most of them neither care about nor understand. The history of the Japanese in the Monterey Bay Region is a transpacific story.

GLOSSARY

It is essential that one understands and knows how to pronounce the following Japanese terms. Understanding these terms is a major element in understanding how the Japanese community views itself.

JAPANESE IMMIGRANT GENERATIONS

Issei ("ee-say"). First generation, the immigrants from Japan. Prohibited from becoming U.S. citizens, they were "aliens ineligible for citizenship" until 1952.

Shin Issei. Means "new" Issei and is often applied to immigrants who came from Japan after 1952.

Nisei ("knee-say"). Second generation, the children of the immigrant generation. In contrast to their parents, the Nisei were American citizens because they were born here.

Sansei ("saan-say"). Third generation. Born after 1945, this generation went to school during the civil rights era of the 1960s and 1970s. This generation is characterized by a high rate of "out marriages," or partners who are not of Japanese ancestry. They were leaders of the redress campaign.

Yonsei ("yone-say"). Fourth generation.

Gosei ("go-say"). Fifth generation.

OTHER TERMS

Kibei ("key-bay"). Nisei who were sent back to Japan for their education. Where many of their fellow Nisei spoke no Japanese, for example, the kibei were often bilingual when they returned.

Nikkei ("knee-cay"). A collective term that means the entire Japanese community, from Issei to new immigrants.

Nihon machi ("knee-hone ma-chee"). Japantown. General term used to describe the Japanese section of a town. Japanese equivalent to Chinatown.

INAPPROPRIATE TERMS

Though it was in common use from the arrival of the Japanese through World War II, the word "Jap" is now highly offensive and inappropriate. It should only be used when quoting historical documents. The word "Nip," a contraction of Nipponese, is also inappropriate and should be avoided.

The term "Oriental" is a vestige of European colonialism and is no longer appropriate when used to describe people or culture. Use of this word is restricted to carpets.

"Far East" is also an inappropriate Eurocentric phrase. Once used to describe East Asia's location in relation to Europe, the phrase tends to lump East Asian countries and cultures together. Geographical terms such as East Asia and Southeast Asia are preferred, and wherever possible one should use the name of the country. "Far East" further confuses the history of East Asians in America, since China and Japan are actually WEST of California. Also, the word "Eastern," when used to denote cultures or religions, should be avoided. One should use the name of the religion, such as Buddhism or Taoism.

For Californians, terms such as "Far East" and "Eastern," should be restricted to discussions about New Jersey, its people and religions.

JAPANESE NAMES

Traditional Japanese name-order is similar to that used in China, with family name first. In this book, the names of historical figures such as Tokugawa Ieyasu are given in traditional order, while names after 1850 are given in the order used in the United States. The name of Gennosuke Kodani of Point Lobos, for example, is given in that order because he used it after he moved to the United States. In Japan, he was known (and still is) as Kodani Gennosuke. The traditional family-first name-order continues as the standard in Japan.

1 CH... REDECESSORS
1850...

The story of the J... egion spans only the last hundred years of the region's history. ... conomic, and political patterns were already set by the 1880s. Fellow i... ed and worked in the region since the 1850s, laying down grooves an... the Japanese when they arrived. The majority of the region's residents ... eir Chinese predecessors, and most of the early impressions were f... re, or were not, like the Chinese. On the other hand, both the Jap... the immigrants themselv... the history of the Chines... ica and often made effort... that would be distinctive ...

Thus it is impossible to ... of the Japanese in the regi... understanding of how the ... it was by the 1880s and the... nese played in its developm...

MONTEREY BAY REG...

As its title suggests, the scope ... the region immediately adjace... Bay, on the central California ... encompasses all of the major ri... drain the counties of Monterey,... and Santa Cruz, along with the... of Santa Clara County. The app... ical unity of the region is compl...

...rry growers, Pajaro Valley, c. 1890. The Chinese were ...e primary farm laborers in the region during the last half of the nine-teenth century.
FLORENCE WAUGAMAN

jumble of mountain ranges that effectively chop the region into a series of micro-regions.

Beginning with the first immigrants into the region over 10,000 years ago, the challenge was to find and develop niches that would support human communities. The diversity of Indian cultures that existed when the Spanish first made permanent settlement in the region in 1770 was eventually overlaid by a similar diversity of European and American immigrants. Monterey was the capital of the province of Alta California during both the Spanish (1770-1822) and Mexican eras (1822-1848).

A decidedly north-south regional division began during the Mexican era when increasing numbers of Yankee and European immigrants moved into the Santa Cruz mountains on the north side of the bay to work in the redwood forests. When gold was discovered in the Sierra Nevada in 1848, the political and economic axis of California shifted out of the region leaving behind a very Hispanic town of Monterey.

By the time California was admitted to the Union in 1850, the bay was bracketed by a Yankee Santa Cruz on the north and a decidedly Hispanic Monterey on the south. Santa Cruz's economy became hitched to the industries of lumber, lime, tanning, and other manufacturing based on the natural resources in the mountains and the dependable perennial streams that drove the wheels of industry.

With neither the dependable water nor the dense redwood forests and mineral deposits, Monterey's economy focused directly on the

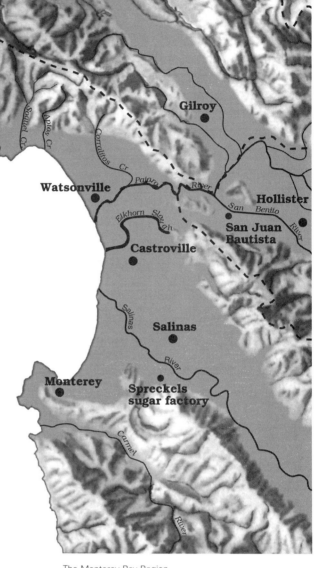

The Monterey Bay Region

adjacent marine resources. The cold, clear coastal waters were a veritable cornucopia of sea life. By the mid 1850s, Monterey's fishing and whaling companies complemented the lumber mills, lime kilns, and tanneries at Santa Cruz.

Asian immigration into the region began in the early 1850s, when Chinese fishermen set up camps on the Monterey side of the bay.

CHINESE IN THE MONTEREY BAY REGION

This introduction focuses on Chinese immigrants to the region for several reasons. First, the Chinese provided some of the inspiration and much of the labor for the region's economic development in the last half of the nineteenth century. The stories of the development of agriculture and fishing and the building of the region's railroads are inseparable from that of the Chinese.

Second, the niches which the Chinese developed were, for the most part, inherited by the Japanese immigrants who followed them. Young Japanese immigrants stepped, almost literally, into shoes that had been filled by Chinese immigrants.

Third, the region's perceptions and understandings of Asian culture were originally learned from Chinese immigrants. The Chinese were the cultural template against which the Japanese were most often compared. Since both groups came from Asia, the Japanese quickly inherited the racism and prejudice that had haunted the Chinese since their arrival. Initially, whites welcomed the Japanese because they were NOT Chinese, but the welcome quickly eroded into anger and outright hostility as the Japanese quickly adapted to the economic and political landscape and became economic competitors.

Fourth, the tools of restrictive legislation that had been used so effectively against the Chinese were sharpened and brought quickly to bear on the Japanese. Whites had learned all they knew about Asians by dealing with the Chinese, and it did not take but a few years for the cry of "the Japanese must go" to replace the earlier motto "the Chinese must go," all along the Pacific Coast.

Finally, the Japanese were very aware of the history of the Chinese in California. And, where possible, they made conscious efforts not to replicate behavior that brought such wrath down upon their Chinese predecessors. At times they even used the Chinese as a foil in hopes that they might avoid the restrictive legislation which seemed continually imminent. They were not successful, however, and by 1924 the Japanese were as excluded from citizenship and immigration as the Chinese.

Jung Family, Pebble Beach, 1880s. One of the rare Chinese families in the Monterey Bay Region.   MONTEREY PUBLIC LIBRARY

CHARACTERISTICS OF CHINESE IN THE REGION

Most of the Chinese who came into the Monterey Bay Region were from villages in the Pearl

River delta near the city of Canton in Southern China. Facing economic hardship caused, in part, by European colonial efforts in Canton and nearby Hong Kong, Chinese emigrants moved across the Pacific to California and the "Golden Mountain." Finding neither success nor a welcome in the Sierra gold fields, many moved to other areas in California to seek their fortunes.

Some, such as the Kwok family of Point Lobos, sailed directly across the Pacific in junks, bringing with them entire households ready to establish a permanent home in the Monterey Bay Region.[1] Except for the Chinese families who settled on the Monterey Peninsula, most of the Chinese immigrants to the region were solitary men who lived in Chinatowns and provided the labor necessary for the area's economic development. Whether it be in manufacturing, agriculture, land reclamation, or railroad construction, the economic wheels of the nineteenth century in the Monterey Bay Region were turned by Chinese muscle.

Their influence was well out of proportion to their numbers, however. Numbering in the dozens in the 1860s, the Chinese population in the region did not exceed 1,000 until 1880, representing just under 4% of the total population. In 1890 the Chinese achieved the largest percentage of total population in the region's history, just under 6%. (For Chinese regional population figures from 1880 through 1990, see Appendix C, pp. 142-143)

ANTI-CHINESE RACISM

The Chinese soon found themselves to be the targets of regular, systematic anti-Chinese racism, which narrowed their world and kept them outside the American mainstream they were helping to create. Feeling safer and more secure in the familiar language and culture of home, most Chinese lived in a transplanted Chinese world, where they often spoke only to other Chinese. Their distinctive language, quilted coats, slippers, and braided queues made them easy targets for racist acts and legislation, and by the 1870s they had become the scapegoats for all the region's ills, both real and imagined.

Generally, the most strident anti-Chinese voices were raised in the industrial area around Santa Cruz, where the Chinese were not a primary source of labor. In the more agricultural cities of Watsonville and Salinas, there was some, albeit reluctant, support for the Chinese, because they were essential to keeping the fields in production. Monterey, itself a multicultural city, had the most muted anti-Chinese sentiment. Not surprisingly, when the Japanese entered the region, they found their strongest opposition in those places where the Chinese had.

Despite the understanding that they were a necessary part of the region's economy, by the late 1870s, no group was more universally disliked than the Chinese. In an 1879 statewide referendum held about continuing Chinese immigration into the United States, of the 5,828 votes cast in the Monterey Bay Region, only seven votes were cast in favor of keeping the door open to Chinese.[2] Since the Chinese could not become naturalized citizens, they were not allowed to vote in the referendum.

LEGAL STATUS AND EXCLUSION

By the late 1870s the Chinese were surrounded by a web of restrictive laws, ranging from those prohibiting their becoming naturalized citizens to local ordinances regulating their conduct and behavior. It is no wonder that so few of the early immigrants felt comfortable enough to bring their wives and families to the United States. One local city went so far as to make it illegal for their Chinese residents to fly kites.[3]

Amazingly, despite the widespread hostility and prejudice that they confronted every day, the Chinese in the Monterey Bay Region found economic niches that allowed them to keep low profiles and still make a living. The Golden Mountain took on a taste of bitterness to the Chinese, but, compared to the chaos that had consumed their homeland, California continued to be a desirable place. As one Chinese scholar who found himself digging ditches in Watsonville wrote in 1871, "I shall...with patience and resignation continue to dig with an abiding hope for something better...."[4] It was that hope for something better that kept them going.

Meanwhile, California's congressional delegation took its opposition to Chinese immigration to Washington D.C., eventually passing, in 1882, the first immigration law in United States history that restricted a particular race.

Top of Workingmen's Party ballot cast in Santa Cruz County, 1879.
SANTA CRUZ MUSEUM OF NATURAL HISTORY

No further immigration of Chinese laborers to the United States was allowed, and after its passage, only merchants and scholars could come to the United States. The exclusion of Chinese was continued until 1943, as was the prohibition of their becoming naturalized citizens. (See Appendix D, pp. 144-147, for an overview of immigration law.)

The Chinese Exclusion Law of 1882 was an important part of the Japanese immigrant story, because once the flow of Chinese immigrants slowed, agricultural interests in California began to look for another source of laborers to take their place.

CHINA'S INTERNATIONAL STATUS

Beginning with the Opium War in 1839 and the signing of the Treaty of Nanking, which ceded Hong Kong Island to Great Britain in 1842, China grew weaker in the face of European colonial expansion. Though China never became a European colony, as did India, for example, it was beset with a series of ignominious wars and defeats, until, by the 1890s, it was hardly able to manage its own internal affairs. Chinese immigrants in the United States did not have a strong international voice to represent them. In the early years, the Chinese government expressed no interest in looking after its emigrants in America. In 1858 a Chinese official noted, "When the emperor rules over so many millions, what does he care for the few waifs that have drifted away to a foreign land?"[5]

Thus, when the "few waifs" from China in the Monterey Bay Region found themselves surrounded by laws and sometimes even mobs, they had to look within their own community organizations for support and strength. This they were able to do through an elaborate pyramid of associations, topped by the Chinese Six Companies in San Francisco.

Also, China was ruled during this period by a non-Chinese minority group from Manchuria. Numerous efforts to overthrow the Manchu government were supported by the Chinese living in the Monterey Bay Region, and Chinese fund-raisers often passed through, hoping to get their overseas brethren to contribute to their cause. Chinese immigrants gave much support to various Chinese causes during the nineteenth century but received little support in return.

China's weak international status in the last half of the nineteenth century stood in marked contrast to the ascendant strength of Japan dur-ing the same period. The Chinese received no assistance from their government, making them even more vulnerable. The Japanese immi-grants, on the other hand, were represented by a government gaining strength and prestige by the day, giving their story here an entirely dif-ferent flavor. When the anti-Chinese forces wished to pass legislation restricting Chinese immigrants, they did so with impunity. The anti-Japanese forces, on the other hand, always had to be aware of an increasingly powerful Japanese government, which took a very close interest in their emigrants in America.

CHINESE FISHING INDUSTRY

The local Indian groups had made extensive use of the region's marine resources, but when their numbers began to drop following the establishment of Spanish occupation in 1770, neither the Spanish nor the Mexicans who fol-lowed had much interest in fishing. Therefore, when the Chinese began arriving in Cali-fornia in the early 1850s, they found the fishing grounds in the Monterey Bay Region almost completely unoccupied. The decimation of the sea otter population by fur hunters dur-ing the Mexican era combined with the general distaste that the local Hispanic and Yankee population had for abalone meant that there were abalone everywhere along the rocky Monterey Peninsula coastline.

The Chinese focused first on the abalone, harvesting the mollusks from the rocks as far

Chinese fishing village and abalone shells, Pebble Beach, c. 1890.   MONTEREY PUBLIC LIBRARY

into the sea as low tides would allow. They then removed the abalone's muscled foot and dried it for shipment to markets in San Francisco and China. Eventually they sold the shells to button and jewelry manufacturers in New England. Apparently the Chinese had neither the desire or technology available to allow them to dive and harvest the abalone that were clearly visible in deeper water around the Monterey Peninsula. The greatest obstacle to the Chinese taking abalone in deeper water was the extremely cold water. The Chinese used long poles to harvest sea urchins from deeper water and even attempted a similar method for getting abalone, though it was not very successful.

Once the larger intertidal abalone were removed, the Chinese shifted their attention to harvesting fish, sharks, and seaweed, the bulk of which was dried and shipped out of the region. By the 1860s there were Chinese fishing villages at several locations around the Monterey Peninsula, with the largest just outside the western city limits of Monterey, at a place called Point Alones.

The Chinese dominated the region's fishing industry into the 1870s, because they had both the drying technology and the market access for their dried fish products. Once a railroad connection was completed to Monterey in 1874, Italian fishermen moved into the region and dominated the fresh fish business. The bay was big enough for both the Chinese and Italians, however, and over the years the Chinese focused and refocused their efforts, as non-Chinese fishermen continued to shadow them.

The strategy that allowed the Chinese fishing industry to survive in the region for over a half century was an important one—they never competed directly with non-Chinese fishermen. Because they had an extremely broad vision about the utility of marine resources, the Chinese shifted their fishing niches to avoid confrontation.

CHINESE IN AGRICULTURE

Beginning with the Spanish period in 1770, the Indians were the agricultural labor mainstay in the Monterey Bay Region. As the Indian people melted away from diseases to which they had no immunity, the Chinese took their place in the fields. Beginning in the late 1860s, Chinese farm laborers became a common sight throughout the Monterey Bay Region, and by the late 1870s, they were the primary source of labor for an ever-diversifying agricultural industry.

The introduction of sugar beets in the 1870s revolutionized the region's agriculture, helping lead it from a cereal grain-dependent industry to a more diversified one by the 1890s. The Chinese dominated the cultivation of sugar beets, and from the industry's small beginnings near Soquel in 1874 to the erection of the huge sugar beet factory in Watsonville in 1888, the Chinese were the labor backbone for the sugar industry. Many Chinese immigrants received their introduction to the region through weeding, thinning, and digging sugar beets.

The expansion of the industry in the 1890s and the erection of Claus Spreckels' huge sugar beet refinery near Salinas in 1898 further emphasized the necessity of a new source of laborers to replace the aging Chinese cut off from China in 1882. As we shall see in Chapter 3, many of the early Japanese immigrants also entered the region through the beet fields.

The Chinese also provided the muscle for other labor-intensive crops during the 1870s and 1880s, including strawberries, hops, tobacco, and fruit orchards.

The Chinese also helped change the physical face of the region by clearing land and grubbing and draining sloughs and swamps. Much of the low-lying land at the mouths of the Salinas and Pajaro Rivers was brought into production by Chinese men willing to undertake the backbreaking labor necessary to clear out the willows and dig the ditches to drain off the standing water.

CHINESE RAILROAD BUILDING

Beginning in the early 1870s, Chinese men provided the labor to build the railroad system that brought the Monterey Bay Region closer to the outside world. For over two decades, Chinese railroad workers were a regular part of the region's landscape, risking life and limb to drape railroad grades over and through the surrounding mountains.[6] Since most of the region's railroad system was complete by 1890,

the Japanese did very little railroad construction. However, as shall be seen, Japanese were sometimes hired by the railroad companies to maintain existing lines.

CHINESE SERVICE

One niche that the Chinese developed almost from their first arrival in the 1850s was providing service to the non-Chinese community. Chinese houseboys, domestics, cooks, and laundrymen became fixtures throughout the region. Most large ranches and logging operations had at least one Chinese cook, while large hotels, such as the Del Monte in Monterey, had large Chinese staffs to serve their patrons. Each community had at least one Chinese laundry, and some, such as Santa Cruz, had upwards of a dozen laundries in the 1880s.

Early Japanese immigrants also moved into these occupations as the aging Chinese left them. Young Japanese students often worked as houseboys to support themselves, and Japanese laundries emerged in most communities by the turn of the century. The only service job that did not seem to attract many Japanese immigrants was camp or ranch cook. For reasons still not entirely clear, and long after Chinese immigra-

Chinese railroad workers, Pacific Grove, 1889.

CALIFORNIA STATE LIBRARY

tion was stopped in 1882, Chinese cooks continued to hold forth in the region's kitchens.

Summary

The region that the Japanese immigrants entered in the late 1880s had reached a stable economic plateau. The completion of the Del Monte Hotel in Monterey (1880) and the opening of the South Pacific Coast Railroad on the north side of the bay in that same year signaled the arrival of high technology and corporate capital. Monterey quickly embraced the upper class tourism promoted by the hotel, while Santa Cruz reveled in the timber boom which exploded in the San Lorenzo River Valley. The region's economy remained healthy throughout the 1880s, and it was against a backdrop of boom and optimism that the first Japanese immigrants arrived in the region.

The Chinese did not share in the optimism of the 1880s. Their exclusion from immigration to the United States in 1882 was followed quickly by increasingly stringent laws such as the 1888 Scott Act, which made it impossible for Chinese who had left the United States to return. China itself was in a steep and steady decline, with the imperial government under attack externally from increasing pressure by European (and eventually Japanese) forces; while internally, Chinese citizens continued to demand governmental reform.

Two Chinese batons were passed by the end of the nineteenth century. In the fields and fisheries of the Monterey Bay Region, the Chinese handed over their jobs to a new group of young Japanese immigrants ready to try their hand at achieving their version of the American Dream. Meanwhile, following Japan's sound defeat of China in the Sino-Japanese War of 1895, Japan emerged as the preeminent power in East Asia.

2 JAPANESE BACKGROUND
TO 1887

The story of the Japanese in the Monterey Bay Region must be seen against the remarkable story of the modernization of Japan. The Meiji renaissance provided the "push" for Japanese emigration. Despite momentous changes in Japan, the culture and values the immigrants brought were very much those of feudal, highly structured Tokugawa Japan. This chapter will develop some of the historical background, but the primary emphasis will be on the culture the Japanese brought to America.

JAPANESE HISTORY

Compared with China's past, Japan's history is linear and tidy. Chinese history is grand vistas measured in thousands of miles; Japanese history is one of subtleties and nuances.

One key to understanding not only the differences between Chinese and Japanese history but also their contrasting world views is in their dissimilar imperial institutions. The beginning of each Chinese dynastic change was marked by complete renewal, an upheaval that saw the destruction of the previous regime (and often the entire ruling family). The last Chinese emperor, who abdicated the throne in 1912, could trace his lineage only to the beginning of the Qing dynasty in 1644.

In Japan, on the other hand, the current Japanese emperor, Akihito, who was installed in 1990, theoretically can trace his lineage back to Japan's mythical first emperor, Jimmu Tenno, in 660 B.C. Admittedly, some unusual twisting

Great Buddha, Kamakura, Japan. Buddhism came to Japan via Korea, where it was adapted to fit the Japanese temperament. Japanese immigrants brought Buddhism to America, where they changed it to fit the American landscape.   ANN LYDON

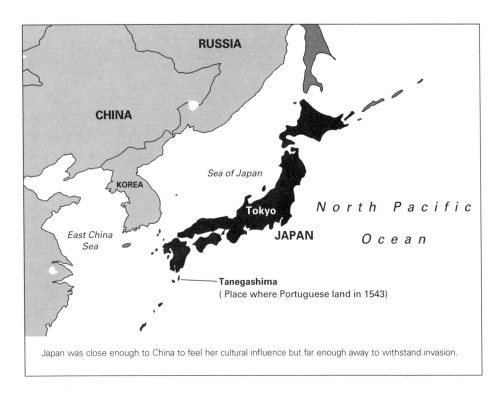

Japan was close enough to China to feel her cultural influence but far enough away to withstand invasion.

invasion by imperial powers (the Mongols came the closest in the late thirteenth century), Japan was near enough to feel the influence of cultural waves. Though Japan was never a Chinese subject state, Japanese culture was heavily influenced by her huge neighbor to the west.

Chinese art, religion, and philosophy, as well as more practical disciplines such as city planning, influenced the Japanese. The Japanese language is filled with Chinese loan words. Perhaps the most visible influence is seen in the written Japanese language, which is composed in part of written Chinese characters called *kanji*. Written Japanese is an excellent example of the adaptive power of the Japanese, who took a written language that had little in common with spoken Japanese and through the force of will made it fit. As a result, Japanese is one of the most complex written languages in the world.

Throughout Japanese history and up to the present time, the Japanese have showed a willingness to examine and explore other cultures. In that respect they were very different from their Chinese neighbors. The Chinese took an almost arrogant position about non-Chinese innovations and ideas: "If we didn't invent it, it can't be important," they seemed to say. The Japanese, however, were quite willing to learn

and turning of history is necessary to make this connection; but Japanese willingness to work so hard to make the link indicates the importance they place in the idea of an unbroken imperial line. The Japanese emperor rarely exercised any real power over the Japanese people, however. When the power shifted away from the emperor, rather than dispatch and replace him, as the Chinese would, the Japanese simply put the new institution beside the throne. Therefore, there were times in Japanese history when power rested three or four stages removed from the emperor.

INNOVATORS

Japan's history reflects a tension between geographical independence and cultural interdependence. Located just far enough off the coast of East Asia to successfully discourage military

new ideas and then, if appropriate, adapt them to the Japanese landscape. They are able to adapt and yet not lose any sense of their uniqueness as a culture.

GUNS

One example of the difference between Chinese and Japanese acceptance of outside innovations can be found in their responses to guns. The Chinese invented gunpowder, using it primarily to make weapons such as bombs and rockets. The invention made its way west to Europe and centuries later returned to East Asia in the form of muskets carried by the Portuguese. The Chinese response to the musket was to dismiss it as a useless "barbarian" idea, a response that ultimately had tragic consequences for the Chinese when Europeans came fully armed in the nineteenth century.

From the moment that guns first arrived in Japan in 1543, the Japanese were fascinated by them. Two Portuguese adventurers aboard a Chinese ship landed on the island of Tanegashima, and Lord Tokitaka, the local feudal master, immediately saw the advantage such weapons would give him in warfare. He purchased the guns from the Portuguese and immediately ordered his swordsmith to begin making copies of them. By 1556 it was estimated that there were 300,000 Japanese-made guns in Japan with another 25,000 having been exported overseas.[1]

Some observers dismiss the Japanese as a people with very little originality—mere copycats. This conclusion misses the point. Japanese culture is resilient and facile, with the Japanese quite willing to add another new layer to their cultural parfait while preserving the older traditions beneath. The Japanese rarely throw anything cultural away. Whether it be the emperor, traditional theater, historic buildings, or even an old tree that has grown tired and wants to fall down, the Japanese will preserve and prop up the old while building something shiny and new beside it.

LIVING TOGETHER IN A SMALL SPACE

In Japan, space is the greatest luxury. Perhaps more than any other people, the Japanese have developed a system that allows them to live together under the most crowded conditions. This dense and homogeneous population (just recently, the non-Japanese population went over 1% for the first time in the history of the country) led to the development of a society that sees itself as one large extended family. Japanese society revolves around respect and civility. Japanese codes of conduct emphasize politeness and respect, traits that are absolutely essential under such crowded conditions. Traditional Japanese houses with interior walls made of paper further emphasize the need for decorum in interpersonal relations. The Japanese are able to live under extremely crowded conditions because of the restraints on behavior imposed by Japanese society.

Square footage is the primary ingredient in determining the value of a Japanese home, and since space is so limited, the Japanese have been forever developing ways to optimize what little space they have. There is no wasted space in Japan, from the farmer who cultivates fields right up to the edge of the field (including roadside rights-of-way and freeway median strips) to the ingenious storage spaces in the typical Japanese household. It is not surprising that the Japanese have led the way in the development of multiuse, space-saving furniture, the futon being the most familiar example in the United States.

JAPANESE LANGUAGE AND THE CULTURE OF THE OBLIQUE

The evolution of the Japanese language was also driven by this feeling of crowding and the familiar. The Japanese language is a model of civility and restraint, helping to round the sharp edges of interpersonal relations. Predictability is essential in Japanese society, while sudden deviations are to be avoided. As in one large family where all members are trying to get along with each other, there can be no rough edges. Conflict and confrontations are to be avoided at all cost. Japanese culture is a culture of avoidance.

What to the Japanese seems extremely civil is often viewed by Americans as excruciatingly vague. Japanese rarely feel the need to communicate constantly as do Americans. There is no need to speak about commonly held emotions. A typical Japanese marriage is often a long silence punctuated by scattered clusters of conversation. Since each partner understands the other perfectly, there is no need to verbalize every little thing. In fact, to a Japanese, a flurry of words often indicates a lack of understanding.

For a Japanese, what often is most important is what is NOT said. This is especially true if the information might bring pain or embarrassment to the hearer. Japanese do not like to say "no." There are many ways to say "no" in Japanese, by saying "yes" but meaning "no."

Ultimately, if a negative answer cannot be avoided, silence is better. For Americans, who are used to the candid and frank exchange of ideas and opinions, this indirection and avoidance can be extremely frustrating.

THE TOKUGAWA AND THE CLOSING OF JAPAN

The arrival of the Portuguese in 1543 was one of the factors leading to a period of warfare in Japan, from which emerged a great unifying family—the Tokugawa. With their center of power in the east, around present-day Tokyo, the Tokugawa eventually brought the warring factions under control and unified the country. The Tokugawa leadership became increasingly nervous about the inroad that Christianity was making on some of its citizens, particularly in the southern part of Japan. In 1613 the government began destroying Christian churches. It wasn't the Christian ideas that concerned the Tokugawa but the possibility that this new organization might affect the important bonds of loyalty that held Japan together.

JAPAN IS CLOSED, 1638

The troublesome Christianity persisted, however, so in 1638 the Tokugawa regime closed Japan. Not only were foreigners prohibited

---

TOKUGAWA LAW REGARDING EMIGRATION - 1638

1) No Japanese ship or boat whatever, nor any native of Japan, shall presume to go out of the country; whoso acts contrary to this shall die, and the ship with the crew and goods aboard shall be sequestered till further order.

2) All Japanese who return from abroad shall be put to death.[2]

from entering Japan, but Japanese citizens were forbidden to have any contact with those who might come ashore accidentally. And Japanese citizens could not leave Japan. Except for a limited window allowing some Dutch and Chinese traders at Nagasaki—neither the Dutch nor Chinese were interested in missionary work—Japan was almost completely isolated from the outside world from 1639 to the 1840s.

TOKUGAWA CULTURE

During the two centuries of isolation, the Japanese were able to focus their energies on their own institutions, defining and refining the rules that influence Japanese society to this day. The culture and values that Japanese immigrants brought to the Monterey Bay Region in the late nineteenth and early twentieth centuries were those of Tokugawa Japan.

Tokugawa Japan was highly organized and restrictive. Rules and regulations bound the individual citizens to their respective positions in society. Anything that might destabilize society was prohibited by Tokugawa law, including ideas from the outside. Citizens of Tokugawa Japan resembled a bonsai tree with each limb bound tightly in place by the wires of Tokugawa law. The system was extremely successful, for just at a time when European culture was making far-reaching inroads into China, for example, Japan was stable, closed and at peace.

LOYALTY AND THE *TALE OF THE FORTY-SEVEN RONIN*

One of the most admired cultural attributes for the Japanese is that of loyalty, a concept that was sharpened and honed in the strict and disciplined world of Tokugawa samurai.

The *Tale of the Forty-Seven Ronin* is the most well known story in Japan, and even though the events took place in the early eighteenth century, the Japanese continue to be touched by it.

A Synopsis: In April 1701 a young and somewhat impetuous Japanese lord, Asano, was required to perform a series of state ceremonies in the Tokugawa palace in Edo (now Tokyo). Asano did not know how to perform them and he sought the advice of an older nobleman named Lord Kira. Kira mocked Asano at every turn, ridiculing him for not knowing the regulations. Asano finally snapped, drew his sword, and slashed Kira across the face. Fighting in the Tokugawa palace was a serious breach of protocol, regardless of the reasons, and Lord Asano was condemned to commit suicide, his property was confiscated, and all the members of his clan were disbanded. (The image of cherry blossoms falling softly while Asano disembowels himself is a favorite in Japanese theater and film.)

Lord Asano's samurai are expected to avenge the death of their lord against Lord Kira, but Kira is expecting it. So instead of proceeding immediately with their revenge, Asano's masterless samurai (the term "ronin" means "wave men") agree to wait until Kira has lowered his guard.

The hero is the leader of Asano's men, Oishi Kuranosuke. Oishi and the other samurai disband and set about their individual lives, with Oishi taking on the persona of a drunken loser, abandoning his family (who did not know of the plot), and moving to Kyoto.

Revenge finally came in January 1703, when Oishi sent out the secret call to his fellow samurai that Kira had relaxed his vigilance and it was time to avenge the death of their young lord. On the snowy night of January 30, Oishi and his forty-six fellow avengers stormed Lord Kira's household grounds and captured him. When Kira refused to commit suicide, Oishi had him decapitated. As dawn broke over Tokyo that winter morning, the surviving ronin walked proudly through the city streets, carrying Kira's head back to Lord Asano's grave at the temple of Sengakuji.

Unfortunately, the act of vengeance was also a capital offense under Tokugawa law, and Oishi and his fellow samurai were required to commit ritual suicide, which they did in February 1703. They were buried beside Asano in the cemetery at Sengakuji, where they lie to this day. Even today a steady stream of visitors come to Sengakuji to pay their respects to the men who put their loyalty to their lord before everything else.

Gravestones of the 47 Ronin, Sengakuji Temple, Tokyo. Visitors come from all over Japan to visit the graves of the loyal samurai.   SANDY LYDON

Each year at the New Year, a new version of the story is produced for Japanese television, and the tale has been adapted in every medium imaginable, from film to books.

The story emphasizes a number of qualities the Japanese continue to admire, most importantly, the surrender of personal well-being to the objectives of the group. The heroes of the story abandoned their families and themselves in the service of their lord.

JAPAN AND AMERICA COMPARED: THE SAMURAI AND THE GUNFIGHTER

One way of understanding the differences between Japanese and American cultures would be to compare their mythic movie heroes. Oishi Kuranosuke is the hero of the *Forty-Seven Ronin* because of his total commitment to the goals of the group. Compare Oishi with the classic American movie heroes depicted in the American West. They wander the landscape alone, often reluctant to commit to anything except some kind of personal code of justice or honor. Whether it be Alan Ladd's "Shane" or Clint Eastwood's steely eyed drifter, we admire their individuality and personal courage. The image of the successful gunfighter riding off into the sunset—alone—is a useful one when compared to the ending of most Japanese samurai stories, where the successful heroes often commit ritual suicide as their final act of commitment to group goals.

JAPANESE FAMILY

The basic unit of Tokugawa society was the *ie*, or "continuing family". The *ie* united ancestors, four living generations (grandparents, parents, children, and grandchildren), and descendants yet unborn. The primary objective of the *ie* was to keep the property intact and the family line unbroken. Ancestors were revered in Japanese society but not worshipped to the extent they were in China.

Each member of the continuing family surrendered his or her individuality to the unit, and all decisions were made in consideration of group goals. The property and continuity of the family was of paramount importance in Japan, even more important than blood relationship or kinship. Adoption was quite common in households where either there was no son or the level of talent among the male offspring was not sufficient to carry the interests of the family forward into the future.

One of the most important parts of the traditional Japanese household system, particularly for the Japanese who emigrated, was the practice of primogeniture. Since Japanese property holdings were rarely large enough to support sprawling extended families, property passed to the eldest son. Younger sons either became employees of the oldest or left the household to start their own. Once separated, the brothers usually became quite distant, their kinship continuing in name only.

The traditional Japanese household system made it relatively easy for Japanese society to modernize. Younger brothers could move to the new urban centers without being hindered by ties or allegiances back in the village. The loyalty could be focused either on their new family or even the "family" of a business.

Remember, Oishi Kuranosuke is a hero because he destroyed his family in order to perform his duty to his deceased lord.

What does the concept of *ie* mean for Japanese immigrants to the United States? Japanese men who came to the United States at the turn of the twentieth century were able to adapt to the new culture they found here, and they came relatively unencumbered by family constraints and ties. This is not to say that they did not care about their families in Japan, but if an opportunity arose to establish a household in the United States, they often took it.

COMPARING CHINESE AND JAPANESE FAMILIES

The ideal traditional Chinese family, *jia,* was an extended, multigenerational household consisting of all the sons, their wives, any unmarried daughters, children, grandchildren, great-

---

JAPANESE, CHINESE, AND AMERICAN VALUES COMPARED

Japanese	Chinese	American
A. Group Reliance	A. Family Reliance	A. Individualism
B. Emphasis on hierarchy	B. Emphasis on hierarchy	B. Emphasis on equality
C. Obligation to family	C. Responsibility to family	C. Obligation to self
D. Dependant	D. Dependant	D. Independant
E. Responsibility to others	E. Responsibility to family	E. Responsibility to self

Chart derived, in part, from John Connor, *Tradition and Change in Three Generations of Japanese Americans.*[3]

grandchildren—as many people as possible under the same roof. Tied together by a common surname and common ancestors, the focus was on the continuity of the family. The Chinese family came first, the family holdings second. Chinese novels, such as Ba Jin's classic *The Family*, revolve around the difficulties posed to the family by change or lack of talent. If the lack of an heir or strife eventually split a family apart, the property was divided equally between the brothers.

The Confucian ethic and imperial law reinforced the importance of the family, and for a Chinese, the loyalty and responsibility to the family was paramount. Loyalty was not easily transferred to anything beyond the family.

Classic Chinese Puzzlement: A son sees his father commit a crime. Does he report the father to the authorities? The Confucian answer to this was a resounding NO. In the Chinese view of things, blood was stronger than law.

Thus, both in terms of culture and family responsibility, it was difficult for a Chinese to leave China. Not only were non-Chinese cultures seen as undeveloped and "barbarian," but the tie to the family back in China was extremely powerful. Combined with the anti-Chinese forces encountered in the United States, the result was Chinatowns—Chinese communities of men thrown together for the moment in alliances and arrangements seen as temporary, useful only until they could be reunited with their families either in the United States or in China.

For the Japanese who came to America, the family was much more fluid and adaptable. Younger sons were expected to start their own households. What difference was there between moving to the new urban center of Tokyo or America? Or Brazil?

The ability to transfer their loyalty to a group other than the family made it easier for the Japanese to adapt once they were here. Labor clubs became surrogate households, with members quickly pledging support for the benefit of the group. In a sense, Japanese laborers came to the United States already organized for collective bargaining. From the beet fields of the Salinas Valley to the cannery wharves of Monterey, the Japanese quickly pooled their resources and drove hard bargains with their employers.

The traditional family often weighed heavily against the efforts of the Chinese in the region. It was difficult for a Chinese immigrant to trust anyone beyond immediate family. As the Chinese immigrants attempted to gain a foothold on this shore, they were always looking over their shoulders, back to the Middle Kingdom, their ancestors, and their family. The Japanese, on the other hand, were much lighter on their feet. And, ironically, when American immigration policy was adopted that made it easy for them to establish families here, they did so with little hesitation.

OTHER TOKUGAWA CULTURAL VALUES

OBLIGATION OR DUTY

The concept of *on* (rhymes with "bone") was the most important concept to come with the Japanese to the United States. Variously defined as respect or duty, *on* was the glue that bound the Japanese community together. The responsibility was reciprocal—a leader had an obligation to the followers and vice versa. Within the Japanese family, the male leadership received *on* automatically, and *on* was also given to people in superior positions outside the family, including teachers and bosses. *On* also could be created by doing someone a favor. The person receiving the favor was obligated by the act to later return the favor.

The concept of *on* can still be seen in the intricate gift-giving within (and outside) the community. The giving of gifts seems to be endless, but there are many different levels of gifts and times that gifts are given.

SHAME

In Japanese culture it was good to bring honor to the family and very bad to bring dishonor. Shame, or *haji,* was the powerful force that kept order in Japanese society. To behave unpredictably or improperly generated shame. Individuals were inhibited by the possibility that their acts might disgrace the family or, on a wider plane, the entire community. Ironically, individual success could bring honor to the family, but the possibility of failure restrained the willingness to take risks. Again, the individual disappeared within a group to avoid the risk of shame. To be personally blamed or held responsible for a failure was just about the worst thing that could happen to a member of the Japanese community. And still is.[4]

EMPEROR MEIJI AND THE OPENING OF JAPAN: 1854-1868

Japan had been isolated for over two centuries when Commodore Matthew Calbraith Perry sailed into Edo Bay in 1854 and invited Japan to enter the mid-nineteenth century. Many Japanese leaders had been watching with concern as China slowly came to be crushed under the European military heel. The Opium War

and humiliating Treaty of Nanking of 1842 stood as a stark example of what could happen if Japan did not set about the process of catching up. After an internal struggle over how to react to the outside threat, Emperor Meiji was restored to the throne (though he had no real power) in 1868, and Japan started playing catch-up.

Japan's history between 1868 and 1905 is an amazing story of a determined nation catching her neighbors and becoming a dominant power in East Asia.

FIRST IMPRESSIONS, 1860

Americans knew little about Japan, and due to the policy of Tokugawa isolation, Japanese knew less about America. In the spring of 1860, the first diplomatic mission from Japan arrived in San Francisco. The daily journals kept by several of the mission members confirm the fascination the Japanese had about American customs and technology. Historian Peter Duus has collected a number of those first impressions, in *The Japanese Discovery of America,* which highlight Japanese efforts to discern how things worked in America.[5] (One of the members of this first expedition was Fukuzawa Yukichi, founder of Keio University. Several of the Japanese pioneers in the Monterey Bay Region graduated from Keio.)

The culture shock experienced by the members of the 1860 mission no doubt was similar to that felt by Japanese immigrants thirty years later. The Japanese found themselves in a topsy-turvy world with no apparent class distinctions or hierarchies to guide them. As one Japanese mission member wrote, "We felt slightly put out of countenance, when we discovered that the Americans attached little importance to class distinction, and dispensed with all manners of decorum."[6] Upon each new discovery, the Japanese noted the method of manufacture:

> Then there was a very unusual dessert. It was made of ice. It was of different colors and shapes and was very sweet. It melted quickly upon being put in the mouth and the taste was good. The name of this is ice cream. In order to make it, it is put in a vessel which is turned in hot water. Then it is put into a churn surrounded by ice.[7]

During later missions, such as the Iwakura Mission of 1871, the Japanese continued to be puzzled by the differences between the two cultures: "What is appropriate deportment for us seems to attract their curiosity, and what is proper behavior for them is strange to us."[8]

EARLY IMAGES OF A MODERNIZING JAPAN

Americans were intrigued with Japan's efforts to modernize, and they watched with fascination as the delegations came and went. And, as the Japanese quickly adopted European culture, local newspapers purred with satisfaction. "The Japanese are fast adopting our clothing and social customs," said the editor of the *Watsonville Pajaronian* in 1872, and local newspapers noted the opening of Christian churches in Japan and the interest that the Japanese had in learning English. The several hundred Japanese students who were studying throughout the United States were "patient, inquiring, and wonderfully hard-working."[9]

A good example of Japan's worldwide search was an expedition that arrived in Salinas in early March 1877. The group consisted of three Japanese men and an American go-between. The Salinas newspaper commented that the Japanese men were "dressed in American fash-

ion and one of them spoke English fluently." They were interested in Jessie Carr's thoroughbred shorthorn cattle, and they were so impressed with them that they purchased a small herd. The same expedition also purchased horses, milk cows, and sheep before returning to Japan. These animals were the nucleus of the modern livestock industry in Japan.[10]

JAPANESE CULTURE AS CURIOSITY

The Japanese had no industrial or modern manufacturing capabilities in the 1870s, but they discovered that Americans had a fascination with traditional Japanese handicrafts. The first load of "Japanese Curios" arrived in the region in 1872,[11] and from then until World War II, Japanese parasols, porcelains, painted fans, and lacquerware were very much part of American fashion. Even when the anti-Japanese movement heated up early in the twentieth century, Japanese art and culture continued to be extremely popular. As we shall see, the Japanese were aware of this dichotomy, often using their culture to help neutralize and diffuse the racism and prejudice they encountered.

FIRST JAPANESE VISITORS IN THE MONTEREY BAY REGION: 1874

The first recorded Japanese in the region were a troupe of Japanese acrobats and jugglers who toured the region in the fall of 1874. Under the leadership of a J.R. Marshal, the dozen Japanese performers were described by Benjamin Kooser, editor of the *Santa Cruz Sentinel,* as "shrewd, quiet little men." Kooser was impressed with the group, declaring them to be "intelligent and well-behaved, speaking good English, and observing closely" as they traveled through the area. He was particularly taken with the interest the Japanese visitors showed in his new printing press, which they "curiously" examined.[12]

Japanese circuses became regular visitors on the regional vaudeville circuit, and they never seemed to fail to entertain and fascinate local audiences well into the 1890s.

JAPANESE IMMIGRATION INTO THE REGION

The rapid changes in Meiji Japan were advantageous to Japan's international reputation, but the changes were also extremely painful to much of Japanese society, particularly the farmers. Thus, even as Japan's economy was expanding under pressures to modernize, it was also creating pressures that would eventually be so discouraging that some Japanese would prefer to try their luck elsewhere in the world.

ECONOMIC DISLOCATION

Someone had to pay for the ambitious programs undertaken by the Meiji government, and in 1873, the primary burden of taxation was shifted to the Japanese farmer. The increasing tax burden, combined with other inflation-generating policies, brought financial disaster to many parts of the Japanese countryside. As Japan began to flex her international muscles, particularly leading up to the Sino-Japanese War of 1894-5, the pressures of taxation were cranked up even higher on the Japanese farmers. There were peasant uprisings throughout Japan, but by far the greatest response by many Japanese was to leave for jobs in the newly industrialized cities, or, perhaps, overseas.

CONSCRIPTION

Another policy adopted in 1873 brought a new responsibility to young Japanese men—compulsory military service. This new policy was revolutionary, for up to this time in Japanese history, the responsibilities for fighting had been restricted—by law—to the samurai. Originally filled with loopholes and exceptions, the

Nisei girls, Santa Cruz, c. 1920. The Issei often used traditional Japanese culture to help diffuse racism and prejudice.
JOHN GOTA

draft law was tightened over the years until, in 1889, there were virtually no exemptions.[13] Just as many of their European counterparts had done, a good number of the early Japanese immigrants to Hawaii and the United States left Japan to avoid the draft. But, a sizable number also returned to Japan to fulfill their military service during the Sino-Japanese War of 1894-5 and the war with Russia in 1905.

PULLS TO THE UNITED STATES

Meanwhile, in the fields and factories of California, the passage of the Chinese Exclusion Act in 1882 threatened to interrupt the dependable supply of laborers from China. It took almost a decade for the effects of the law to be felt in the Monterey Bay Region, but American and European labor contractors began to lobby the Japanese government to relax its ban on the emigration of laborers. (Students and acrobatic troupes had come to the United States on special emigration permits issued by the Japanese government.)

A POWERFUL JAPAN

Part of the Japanese government's reluctance to allow emigration was the fear that Japanese citizens would encounter the same hostility and discrimination that Chinese immigrants had encountered both in Hawaii and California. Certainly the government was indeed concerned about the welfare of its citizens overseas, but the overriding motivation was the possible negative effects which such incidents would have on Japan's image in the Pacific and throughout the world.

This sensitivity about international image caused the Japanese government to keep a strong hand on emigration to the United States, up until the United States took the initiative and excluded Japanese immigrants in 1924. The Japanese government not only carefully monitored the issuance of permits and passports to those wishing to leave but also took an overt role in the development of overseas industries and the placement of Japanese laborers in those industries. Where Chinese immigrants were very much on their own once they left China, Japanese immigrants were followed closely by an interested government. And, as Japan's military stature grew in the early twentieth century, this interested Japanese government was also a very powerful one. The presence of a burgeoning military strength just across the Pacific gives the story of the Japanese in America and the Monterey Bay Region a very international flavor. In the early years it was difficult for local observers to see the Japanese and not be reminded of the Japanese fleet just across the horizon on the western side of the Pacific.

EMIGRATION LEGALIZED, 1885

Finally, after considerable efforts from foreign labor contractors (especially those from Hawaii), the Japanese government relented and allowed its citizens to emigrate in 1885. For the first decade the Japanese government itself arranged the labor contracts, and Japanese laborers were one of the country's early exports. When private Japanese companies were allowed to get into the labor contracting business in 1894, the government continued its interest in the Japanese citizens working and living in the United States.[14]

SUMMARY

Though Japan was in the midst of a frenzy of modernization at the time that its emigrants began to come to the United States, the cultural values they brought were very much the products of the feudal Tokugawa period which had just ended. It is difficult to imagine a culture more distinct from that of nineteenth-century America than the culture of Tokugawa Japan. These differences were further complicated by the half-century of exposure that Americans had to Chinese immigrants.

Though they shared the shores of a common ocean, the residents of the Monterey Bay Region had little else in common with the groups of Japanese immigrants who began arriving in the 1880s. Forty years of diplomatic contact between the United States and Japan had brought little solid cultural understanding to the individual households of either place. Historian Peter Duus has written that in the nineteenth century the two countries were separated by a "cultural chasm that at times seemed nearly impossible to span." Separated by languages that shared neither common origins nor writing systems, the cultures of America and Japan differed on almost all the important issues, from the status of the individual to the role of women.[15]

Perhaps the greatest misunderstanding which Americans had about the early Japanese was misreading their willingness to adapt. Though the Japanese quickly adopted American dress and outward social customs, they continued to be Japanese (a fact compounded by their inability to become naturalized American citizens). Both felt betrayed: the Japanese because the promises of wide-open opportunity for all proved to be false; the Americans because these new immigrants continued to be different despite their adaptations.

3 FIRST BEGINNING
1887 TO 1907

The first Japanese immigrants to the United States were students, followed by laborers and some professionals. Initially, Japanese immigrants came into the Monterey Bay Region as farm laborers to take the places of Chinese who were dying, returning to China, or moving to San Francisco's Chinatown. Early Japanese were also employed as woodcutters in the region's forests and as railroad laborers. Japanese fishermen carved out niches in both fishing and abalone diving as well as provided leadership in the developing fish canning industry on the Monterey Peninsula.

Unfortunately, the Japanese also inherited from the Chinese the legacies of racism and prejudice. They became targets of an organized anti-Japanese movement almost from the moment they arrived.

Japanese abalone divers, Point Lobos, c. 1897. These divers quickly learned that their traditional diving clothing was not suited for the extremely cold ocean water off Northern California. PAT HATHAWAY

THE FIRST JAPANESE IN THE REGION: PORTER GULCH, 1887

The first documented Japanese immigrants (as opposed to circus troupes and visiting delegations) were a pair of Japanese nurserymen employed by the Grover Company in the Santa Cruz mountains just east of Soquel in 1887. Brief newspaper references describe a plantation consisting of thousands of trees and vines being laid out in Porter Gulch. Many of the plants were imported directly from Japan, and the two Japanese were hired to cultivate them.[1] As there is no further mention of this experiment, we do not know what happened to the orchards or the two men.

CENSUS OF 1890

The federal census of 1890 lists nineteen Japanese living in Santa Cruz County, one in Monterey County, and none in San Benito County. Because the manuscript census schedules were destroyed in a fire, there is no record of who the twenty Japanese were or exactly where they lived. Based on the census of 1900, one can assume that most of the nineteen in Santa Cruz County were young men living in the Pajaro Valley. And, given the seasonal nature of agriculture, they were probably *buranke-katsugi,* or "blanket men," who carried blankets over their shoulders and moved from one crop to another.

("*Buranke*" is derived from the English word "blanket.")

ISSEI PIONEER: SAKUZO KIMURA

Most historians use the year 1892 to mark the beginning of Japanese residence in the Pajaro Valley and credit Sakuzo Kimura with being the valley's first permanent Japanese resident. (This fact is also recorded on Kimura's grave marker in Watsonville's Pioneer Cemetery.) Originally from Osaka, Kimura arranged for Japanese laborers to enter not only the fields of the valley but also the forests of the Santa Cruz mountains, where they worked as firewood cutters and tanbark choppers.[2]

Kimura is credited with establishing the first Japanese labor club in the Pajaro Valley in December of 1893. The labor clubs became a

Sakuzo Kimura Funeral, 1900. Watsonville

BILL TAO

standard feature of the Japanese American landscape, providing, for a fee, housing and placement for immigrant men. Kimura arranged labor contracts in both the Pajaro and San Juan Valleys during the 1890s. Little is known about Kimura's life before his coming to the Pajaro Valley, but he apparently had traveled widely throughout the world and his command of English was quite high. There is a tantalizing reference to his being either employed by or a member of the U. S. Navy, but this fact has not been confirmed.

Kimura became very ill in March 1900 and died two months later. Kimura was buried in the Catholic section of the Watsonville cemetery, suggesting that he might have been a Roman Catholic.[3]

Taking the Place of the Chinese

In 1893 the editor of the *Watsonville Pajaronian* observed that there had been a "steady encroachment" of Japanese into positions once held entirely by Chinese laborers. Noting that many Pajaro Valley employers preferred the Japanese to the Chinese, the editor concluded that the Japanese were "readily becoming a prominent factor in the labor field of this district...."[4]

The new Japanese labor contractors did not hesitate to underbid the older, more experienced Chinese competitors for the contracts to grow sugar beets. As one newspaper editor described it, the Japanese were "waging war against the Chinese for beet contracts," lowering the farmers costs for raising their beets.[5] Alongside the younger Japanese crews, the steady, dependable Chinese workers looked old and slow. Though they had pioneered the sugar beet contracting business back in the 1870s, in the 1890s the Chinese found themselves outhustled at every turn.

The movement of the Japanese into the sugar beet fields was slowed by the depression that followed the Panic of 1893. The movement in the years 1894 and 1895 of unemployed white laborers into some of the region's beet fields helped retard the need for Japanese laborers; but by 1896, as the economy began to strengthen, the whites left the fields and the Japanese took their places. By 1896 the Watsonville newspaper estimated that there were four hundred Japanese farm laborers in the valley, most of them working in sugar beets.

Kimura Grave, Watsonville

SANDY LYDON

The 1900 federal manuscript census schedules provide the best evidence of the effects of the Chinese Exclusion Law and the impact of these new immigrants from Japan. Of the 950 Japanese in the three counties, 761, or 80%, were agricultural laborers. The average age of the Japanese farm laborers was twenty-seven years, while the average age of the Chinese farm laborers counted that year was fifty-four—exactly double.

The editor of the *Watsonville Pajaronian* summarized it in September of 1900:

> Each year brings out more clearly the imperative need each Fall of plenty of laborers to quickly harvest the orchard and field crops of the Pajaro Valley. Chinese labor is rapidly becoming scarcer. The exclusion act has kept out immigration of young Chinese, and most of those who were in California when the exclusion act was passed have reached an age where they are unable to give a full day's labor. The Japanese have been plentiful, but they are scarce this year, and they are unreliable. They are apt to strike or to jump a job when most needed....[6]

Two months later the same newspaper observed: "[The Japanese] are now more numerous than Chinese in the Pajaro Valley."[7]

HONORING CONTRACTS

Given the reputation that Japanese Americans now have for honesty and commitment, there is a temptation to dismiss the charge that the early Issei were "unreliable" as either a misunderstanding or, at worst, racism. The complaint about unfulfilled contracts and dishonesty was made often during this period, however, and provides a good example of how the larger Japanese community responded to unacceptable behavior from some of its members.

The early years of Japanese agricultural labor contracting have been labeled as "laissez-faire" by historian Yuji Ichioka. It was a rough and tumble time when unscrupulous Japanese labor contractors stole laborers from fellow contractors, undercut each other in contract negotiations, and sometimes even ran off with the money which was due to their laborers. Labor contractors absconding with funds was so common that the Japanese even had a special word for it. [8] (It should be noted that Chinese labor contractors were also sometimes guilty of stealing from their workers.)[9]

There are enough specific regional examples to suggest that there was some truth to the complaint. Local newspaper accounts in 1905 described several instances where Japanese labor contractors promised more laborers than they could deliver. The Silliman family negotiated a contract for 175 laborers to pick and cut apricots, but when the fruit was ripe enough to begin the operation, only 50 men showed up. C. E. Bowman of Corralitos was promised 35 men to work in his orchards, but only four arrived on the appointed day.[10]

Unfortunately for the general Japanese community, the actions of a few labor contractors tarred the entire community with the brush of "unreliability." When the anti-Japanese movement heated up after 1905, the fact that most of the difficulty was actually caused by a few labor contractors was forgotten.

Watsonville apple grower Luke Cikuth remembered the early years of Japanese labor contracting:

> But in [the] early days you couldn't depend on the Japanese to work for you when they said they would. Maybe they didn't understand the language, but no matter what kind of contract you made, you couldn't depend on them. If you

needed some Japanese, you'd say you needed, well, twenty of them to go to work, to pick apples or whatever you wanted them to do. They'd say all right, they'd come. The next morning probably you'd have two or three.

Cikuth went on to explain that, once the growers complained to the U. S. government about the behavior, the Japanese government was notified. "From then on, boy, when the Japanese told you something it was as good as gold."[11]

With the advent of the Japanese associations during the first decade of the twentieth century, honest labor contractors and the Japanese government worked to bring the dishonest contractors into line. Measures such as publishing the pictures and home addresses of renegade contractors in immigrant newspapers, or contacting the home village or town in Japan from which the contractors emigrated had the

desired effect of bringing some order to the business. [12] By 1915, as Cikuth noted, the unscrupulous contractors had been driven out of the business, and the word of a Japanese labor contractor was "good as gold."

JAPANTOWN, WATSONVILLE

Watsonville's early Japanese community had its beginnings across the Pajaro River in the Chinatown known as Brooklyn. Owned by John T. Porter, the Brooklyn Chinatown had been located on the south side of the river (and in Monterey County) since 1888. The earliest Japanese resident of that place was noted in the local newspaper in 1889, and several businesses to service the Japanese laborers began there in the 1890s. The first rental agreement appearing in the Porter family's records is one with a Mr. Katamura, at the southerly end of Brooklyn Street in 1901.[13] Japanese residents remained in the Brooklyn Chinatown up to World War II, and even today, Yagi's Barbershop on Salinas Road serves as a reminder that the Japanese presence across the river has been, except for the wartime removal, continuous.

But the Japanese also made an early statement about their unwillingness

Watsonville, c. 1920. The Japanese first lived in Chinatown on the south side of the Pajaro River (bottom), but soon moved across the river into a Japantown located above and to the right of the bridge.

PAJARO VALLEY HISTORICAL ASSOCIATION

to be grouped together with the Chinese by establishing some of their early bunkhouses and labor clubs on the Watsonville side of the river at the north end of Main Street, on Brennan Street, on Lake Avenue, and at the south end of Main Street. The Japanese refusal to confine their activities to the "other" side of the Pajaro River annoyed the white community in Watsonville. In 1902 the editor of the local newspaper complained about the "ease with which the Japanese have moved in [to Watsonville]…. The quarters of the Asiatics should be outside our city's limits."

By 1910 there was a small, active Japantown centered on the block bounded by Bridge Street on the north, Main and Union Streets on either side, and the river on the south. There were also several Japanese businesses on the north end of Chinatown, across the river. The buildings included labor clubs, churches, grocery stores, boardinghouses, bathhouses, and other businesses designed to service the growing Japanese community.

CLAUS SPRECKELS MOVES HIS FACTORY TO THE SALINAS VALLEY

Claus Spreckels
MUSEUM OF ART AND HISTORY

Working in the sugar beet fields was the entry-level employment for most of the Japanese immigrants in the region. Planting, thinning, weeding, harvesting, and topping sugar beets was very labor-intensive. As the beet acreage moved slowly south from the Pajaro to the Salinas Valley, the Japanese beet workers followed it. Even Claus Spreckels had to acknowledge that it no longer made good economic sense to ship most of the beets back to Watsonville, and in 1898 he built a new sugar factory beside the Salinas River south of Salinas.[14]

The Watsonville newspaper noted in 1897 that "squads" of Japanese laborers were leaving the Pajaro Valley to work in the Salinas Valley.[15] It was estimated that about two hundred Japanese had joined the Chinese and others working the beets in the Salinas Valley that year.[16]

Half of the 761 Japanese farm laborers listed in the 1900 census were working in the fields around Castroville, vivid testimony to the fact

Spreckels sugar factory under construction, 1898. The factory followed the sugar beet acreage into the Salinas Valley, pulling many of the Japanese beet workers along with it.   MONTEREY COUNTY LIBRARY

that the center of sugar beet cultivation had moved from the Pajaro Valley into the Salinas Valley. Over the next decade the beet acreage continued to move south up the Salinas Valley, and the laborers followed the beets.

JAPANTOWN, SALINAS

By 1900 there was a small Japanese service community growing up on Lake Street, just north of the much larger Salinas Chinatown. It was around this original nucleus that Salinas' Japantown eventually developed.

SAN JUAN

Japanese farm laborers also moved into the San Juan Valley to replace the aging Chinese in the 1890s. In 1896, Sakuzo Kimura, the labor contractor from Watsonville, placed Japanese crews to work the sugar beets planted near San Juan Bautista.[17] Kichigoro Tanimura is most often credited with being the first Japanese resident of San Juan Bautista. Tanimura came to the United States in 1896 at the age of twenty-two and by 1900 is listed as living in San Juan Bautista along with five

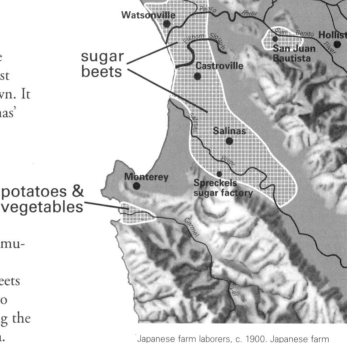

Japanese farm laborers, c. 1900. Japanese farm laborers followed the spread of sugar beets into the Salinas Valley.

Japantown, Lake Street, Salinas, c. 1910. Like most other Japantowns in the region, this one also grew up beside an older Chinatown.

other Japanese. By 1902 Japanese farmers were renting land in the valley to grow berries. [18]

The big turning point in the history of the Japanese in the San Juan Valley came in 1910, when the Ferry-Morse seed company purchased several large tracts of farmland and began growing flowers for seed. Several other seed companies, including one owned by Waldo Rohnert, followed suit, pushing the total acreage of seed flowers to over 2,000 acres.[19] Almost half of the 282 Japanese in San Benito County in the 1910 census were working at the seed farms.

San Juan's small Japantown began to take shape around 1910 at the southeast end of Third Street. There was a pool hall, a barbershop, and a small grocery operated by Tanimura. Behind the grocery store was a large Japanese-style bath, which Tanimura allowed his customers to use free of charge.

San Juan's Japantown grew steadily into the 1920s as Japanese farmers moved into the San Juan Valley.[20]

JAPANESE ON THE MONTEREY PENINSULA

The first recorded instance of Japanese immigrants on the Monterey Peninsula was in 1895, when a group of men led by Otosaburo Noda came to clear brush and trees from the Pacific Improvement Company's property on the southwest side of the peninsula. A native of Saga Prefecture, the thirty-year-old Noda had come into the region in 1885 and worked in the Salinas and Pajaro Valleys. He came to the Monterey Peninsula from Watsonville with several other men to fulfill a contract to cut firewood and clear brush in the pine woods south of Pacific Grove.

Tradition further suggests that he joined a small group of fishermen from Wakayama Prefecture in 1896, organizing them into a part-time fishing company, part-time woodcutting company.

FIRST JAPANESE FISHERMEN

Just as the 1900 census shows the transition from Chinese farm labor to Japanese, so does the same census show the transition from Chinese fishermen to Japanese. Some of the early Japanese fishermen lived within the Point

Alones fishing village on the edge of Pacific Grove.

A second group of twelve Japanese males, which includes two students, four laborers, and six fishermen, is listed in New Monterey. This group's closest neighbor was capitalist John McAbee, the owner of the Arena Gorda Beach. On the hillside above the beach was a neighborhood of Azorean fishermen. This group of Japanese fishermen at McAbee Beach was the predecessor of the later Chinatown that developed there following the May 1906 fire which destroyed most of the Point Alones Chinese fishing village.[21]

JAPANESE ON THE MONTEREY PENINSULA, 1900

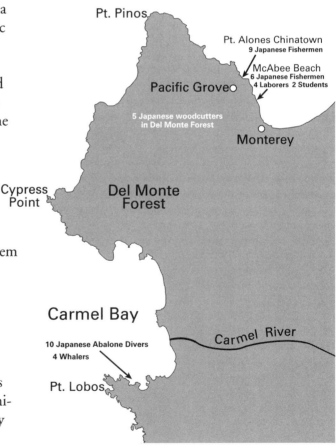

PROFILE: OTOSABURO NODA

Otosaburo Noda was one of the leaders of the region's early Japanese communities. He was instrumental not only in developing local agriculture and fishing but also in providing a visual presence, by building the famous Japanese Tea House on Lover's Point in Pacific Grove.

Otosaburo Noda   SADA ONOYE

1866

Born in Taku, Saga Prefecture. Birth surname was Ishii, but took the name of his sister's second husband, Noda.

1885

Came to San Francisco at age 19.

1885 - 1895

Farmed throughout central California with some success in and around Castroville and Watsonville.

1895

First came to Monterey with Sudano and Imashiro to cut wood for Pacific Improvement Company.

1896

Joined together with small group from Wakayama-ken to start fishing business. Half-time woodcutters, half-time fishermen.

1896

Noda contacted Japanese Agriculture and Commerce Department about the abundant abalone.

1897

Helped found abalone diving industry at Point Lobos

1902

Formed partnership with Harry Malpas and opened Monterey Fishing and Canning Company to can salmon and abalone.

1904

Began building Japanese Tea House on Lover's Point, Pacific Grove. (Tea House torn down in 1918.)

1907

Went to Washington to discuss educational and immigration issues with President Roosevelt.

1910

Involved with Livingston Japanese colony in San Joaquin Valley

1912

One of first successful rice farmers in Colusa County.

1915

Died, April 23, age 49.

Abalone shells at Point Lobos. Noda's notifying the Japanese government about the abalone along the coast resulted in the development of the Japanese-dominated abalone industry.   PAT HATHAWAY

The largest group of Japanese on the Monterey Peninsula in the 1900 census was the ten fishermen and four whalers listed as living at Point Lobos in the spring of 1900. Noda is not listed as living at Point Lobos, but he was largely responsible for the Japanese being there.

In 1896, while working with the woodcutters and fishermen on the Monterey Peninsula, Otosaburo Noda saw the abundant abalone along the rocky shores. Noda sent word of this abalone opportunity to the Japanese government's Agriculture and Commerce Department, and the department eventually asked Gennosuke Kodani, then engaged in the abalone industry in Chiba Prefecture, to consider going to California to investigate.

CHIBA CONNECTION

For Kodani and other abalone fishermen on the Boso Peninsula, the word of California's abalone arrived at a very opportune time—the abalone industry in Chiba was in a shambles. An unusual series of heat waves, beginning in

Gennosuke Kodani   KODANI FAMILY

1892, had killed much of the coastal kelp and with it most of the abalone, and by the mid-1890s, many of the Chiba divers were forced to find work in other areas of Japan. The Chiba economy was also hurt by the government's higher taxes at the successful completion of the war against China, in 1895.

The event that seems to have finally tipped the equilibrium for the Chiba abalone men was a fire in January 1897 which destroyed 30% of the homes in the village of Chikura. Kodani applied for and received a passport in September of 1897 and came to California to find out about the abalone diving possibilities.

Apparently it did not take Gennosuke Kodani long to see the possibilities for abalone diving in the Monterey area, because in December of 1897 his brother Chujiro left Japan for California, accompanied by three Chiba divers.

Gennosuke and Chujiro Kodani were "Meiji men," products of the great awakening that Japan was undergoing in the latter half of the nineteenth century. Gennosuke received a progressive education at Fukuzawa Yukichi's Keio Gijuku (later named Keio University), which included a course of study in marine biology and fisheries management. His younger brother, Chujiro, was the third graduate of the

Abalone Divers with Goggles, Point Lobos, c. 1897   PAT HATHAWAY

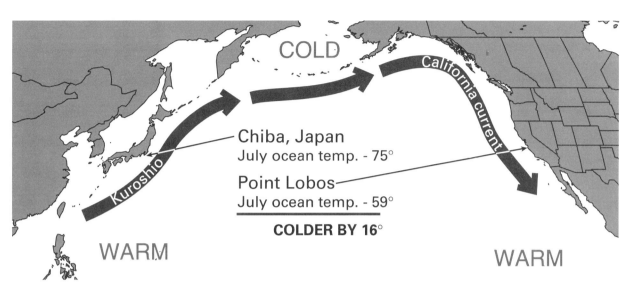

The use of diving helmets and suits was inspired by the extremely cold ocean temperatures off the Monterey Peninsula.

Japan Fisheries Institute, in 1891. Both Kodanis were on the cutting edge of commercial fishing technology in Japan, though neither of them were actually divers themselves.

CHIBA ABALONE DIVING TRADITION

The abalone diving industry had a centuries-long history along the Japanese coast. Traditionally, the diving had been carried out by free-diving men and women using goggles and their lungs to dive for not only abalone but also urchins and other creatures on Japan's coastal shelf.

Deep water diving with the assistance of helmets was developed in Germany in 1839, passed to England, and then traveled to Japan in the 1870s. By the end of the 1870s, the Yokohama Diving Apparatus Company was making helmets and pumps that were used primarily for underwater construction and repairing ships. Mankichi Masuda is credited with being the first to adapt modern diving apparatus to the abalone industry, in April of 1878, in Nemoto village on the Boso Peninsula. The use

of helmets and pumps increased the amount of time that divers could spend on the bottom. Hard-hat diving became the specialty of men, while free diving continued to be practiced by both men and women. (Today along the Chiba coastline hard-hat diving is exclusively a man's occupation, while free diving is practiced by women.) Since the water along the Japanese coastline is relatively warm, the helmets and suits were used primarily to harvest abalone at greater depths, not necessarily to provide warmth to the divers.

FIRST HARD-HAT ABALONE SEASON AT POINT LOBOS: 1898

According to Gennosuke Kodani's son, the late Seizo Kodani, the three divers who came to Point Lobos with Chujiro found the waters off Point Lobos to be too cold. Even with several layers of cotton clothing on their bodies and heads, the divers were so cold that they sometimes refused to go into the water. The Kodanis sent word back to Chiba, and in late 1898 another group of divers arrived, this time with

ABALONE DIVING AT POINT LOBOS, 1905

Helmets, suits, and gear were all imported from Japan. Equipment limited dives to no more than twenty feet of water.

Coal Chute. This coal chute and bunker were left from earlier efforts to mine and ship coal from Point Lobos.

Boat driver and sculling oar. The abalone boats were propelled by a long, sweep oar suspended over the stern. The sculler's job was to keep the boat poised above the diver despite wind and currents.

Japanese diving village included the home of Gennosuke Kodani, the manager, and his family, but also a bunkhouse for the Japanese divers (whitewashed building).

Gennosuke Kodani, graduate of Keio University in Japan, was the driving force behind the abalone diving business on the Monterey Peninsula. In partnership with A.M. Allan he successfully pioneered the industry.

Ex-whaler, Azorean Jacinto DeAmaral worked for the Japanese diving company, demonstrating the multicultural nature of the company as well as the demise of shore whaling.

Abalone boats were recycled New Bedford whale boats adapted for the new technology.

Brass diving pump. All the equipment on the abalone boat was imported from Japan, including the vital air pump, which, when operated by two men, would pump air down to the diver.

PHOTO CREDIT: ROY CHRISTIAN

helmets, marking the beginning of the modern abalone diving industry on the Pacific coast of North America.

The first efforts at establishing the abalone industry were not financially successful either for Noda, who was an early partner in the business, or for other Japanese entrepreneurs, including the Kodanis and Hyakutaro Ide, another immigrant Japanese capitalist. Eventually, at the turn of the century, a partnership

Japanese immigrants were eager to try new things. Issei practicing his bike riding on the Monterey Peninsula, c. 1910.   JOHN GOTA

between Gennosuke Kodani and Alexander M. Allan, the owner of Point Lobos, emerged and began to have some success.

Initially the abalone that were harvested from the base at Point Lobos were dried and shipped to Japan and China or sold in the domestic market in California. The red abalone were quite large, however, and it was not easy to know just when the abalone were properly dried (too damp and they spoil, too dry and they are too hard to cut). So, the men involved in the abalone drying business were eager to find a way to preserve their catch in cans. Several turn-of-the century efforts to can abalone eventually resulted in Kodani and Allan forming the Point Lobos Canning Company.[22]

ACCULTURATION + ADAPTATION = COMPETITION

The early Japanese immigrants were quick and eager students of American culture. They bought and wore the latest American fashions, went to school to learn English, and celebrated the Fourth of July each year in increasing numbers. American flags were displayed prominently alongside those of Japan, and over the years, the American flag grew larger and the Rising Sun disappeared.

During the early years, when Japanese immigrants bought and wore American clothing, it was good news for the non-Japanese merchants. The Chinese had rarely patronized non-Chinese businesses. When early Japanese immigrants came into local dry goods stores to purchase their new American trousers, local business owners were pleased.

The Japanese also moved quickly from being farm laborers to lease holders. Some were able to purchase their own farms within a decade of their arrival in the Pajaro Valley, a feat few Chinese had been able to achieve in half a century.

By 1905 the Japanese began to replicate the local community on a smaller scale in Japantown. As one observer in Santa Cruz County noted:

> When the Japanese arrived in the Pajaro Valley they were welcomed by the merchants largely on account of the fact that they wore American clothing and showed a decided disposition to trade along American lines and rented houses without herding together as do the Chinese. Today the merchants bitterly complain that the Jap has become their very close competitor. He also runs restaurants, barber shops, billiard halls, saloons, groceries, dry goods and ready-made clothing stores in the city of Watsonville, and operates buses and delivery wagons in the adjacent territory.[23]

Stylish Issei tennis players, Watsonville, c. 1915. Tokazo Oda is on the right.   BILL TAO

COMPETITION

The Japanese were not afraid to compete with Chinese or white businessmen. The Chinese had been criticized for their unwillingness to adapt to American customs and ways. They stayed together, preserved their languages, and rarely took part in the affairs of the community. (Of course, they were aliens ineligible for citizenship and thus unable to fully participate in American society.)

The Japanese came to play the American game. They learned the rules, put on the uniform, and stepped out on the field. Their ability to work together and bargain collectively often gave them the advantage. And all of a sudden they had left their "place."

Some even went so far as to apply for American citizenship. In 1900 there were five applications for citizenship from Japanese on the desk of the clerk of Santa Cruz County.[24] Over four hundred Issei on the Pacific Coast successfully naturalized between 1892 and 1906, before federal statute was sufficiently clarified to exclude the Japanese from the process.[25]

The Chinese were chastised when they did not Americanize, and the Japanese were abused when they did. And it certainly did not help that the anti-Chinese movement was so fresh in the minds of white California.

Issei women, Watsonville, 1911. Left to right, Fuji Nakashiki, Kiyo Okita, and Natsu Tao. Issei women quickly discarded their traditional Japanese clothing for modern American dresses and hats.   BILL TAO

The editor of the *Watsonville Pajaronian* summarized it well in 1905:

> It requires but a casual glance at the lower end of Main Street to ascertain that the Japanese colony in that district is almost as numerous and quite as opulent as the old Chinatown which we were so glad to get rid of....Isn't it worthwhile to begin restricting the privileges of these aliens who have no desire to become Americanized except to the extent which permits them to enter into competition with the Americans, whose blood can never be made to assimilate with that of the yellow men of Asia?[26]

ANTI-JAPANESE MOVEMENT AND RESTRICTION OF IMMIGRATION

The anti-Japanese movement was patterned after the organized opposition to the Chinese, which had effectively stopped Chinese immigration following passage of the Chinese Exclusion Act of 1882. Organized anti-Japanese activities began during the depression of the mid-1890s and were very similar in tone and strategy to anti-Chinese efforts. In fact, Denis Kearney, unofficial leader of the movement to restrict Chinese immigration in the 1870s and 1880s, started as early as 1892 to warm up the anti-Japanese fires. At the most basic level, one could take the anti-Chinese rhetoric and simply substitute the word "Japanese."

But the movement against the Japanese also had its origins in the international arena, and in that respect it was very different. Beginning with her defeat of China in 1895, Japan became a major military power in the Pacific, causing considerable fear and hostility on the Pacific Coast. Ironically, Japan's military prowess also helped restrain the anti-Japanese forces in California. Therefore, the restriction

of Japanese immigration was approached with great diplomacy and delicacy by the federal government. President Theodore Roosevelt spent a good deal of time trying to get California to tone down its anti-Japanese rhetoric, fearful that too many inflammatory statements might provoke a war.

One could say that the style with which Japanese immigration was restricted by the federal government was very indirect and discreet—very Japanese.

EARLY REGIONAL ANTI-JAPANESE SENTIMENT

The enthusiasm with which newspaper editors in the Monterey Bay Region watched the early Japanese immigrants move into the fields and adopt American dress and customs began to subside as the depression of the mid-1890s took hold. As early as 1893, the editor of the *Watsonville Pajaronian* wondered whether or not the addition of the Japanese to the Pajaro Valley was a good thing. And though there were no anti-Japanese organizations in the region before 1900, there seemed to be a consensus that the Japanese were as much, if not greater, a threat to the regional community than had been the Chinese.

JAPAN TAKES CONTROL OF ITS EMIGRATION

Always sensitive about its international image and reputation, the Japanese government was quick to respond to anti-Japanese sentiment on the west coast of the United States. In 1900 Japan voluntarily stopped issuing new passports to laborers destined for the United States mainland. Passports continued to be issued to laborers destined for Hawaii, however; between

1900 and 1907, the primary avenue for Japanese headed for California and the Monterey Bay Region was via Hawaii.[27]

TEDDY ROOSEVELT AND THE RUSSO-JAPANESE WAR

Japan's increasing military power in East Asia was demonstrated in a confrontation with Russia in Manchuria, which began in 1904. Both Russia and Japan wanted control of Northeast China and Korea, and the showdown began in and around Port Arthur, the primary shipping port on the Manchurian coast.

The impending war with Russia caused the Japanese government to call all draft-age Japanese citizens, including those living overseas. Several hundred Issei from throughout California had answered the call by early 1904, and

President Teddy Roosevelt speaking in Santa Cruz, May 1903. He is standing in the back of a carriage just to the left of the flag bunting.   MUSEUM OF ART AND HISTORY, SANTA CRUZ

throughout that year regional newspapers noted the departure of local Japanese residents bound for the war. It is interesting to note that public opinion in the city of Santa Cruz was on the side of Japan, since it was believed that Japan had not been been treated fairly by Russia following the Sino-Japanese war. And yet, the newspaper also hoped that the war might attract many Japanese back to Japan, so diminishing the Japanese population in Santa Cruz. [28]

When news of the Japanese victory over the Russians at Port Arthur reached the Pajaro Valley, the local Japanese community was joined by many white celebrants at the Watsonville Opera House.[29]

Then the Russians made the mistake of sending their Baltic fleet all the way around Asia, where the Japanese navy lay waiting for them. On May 27, 1905, the Russian fleet was destroyed in the Battle of Tsushima Strait, and soon thereafter President Theodore Roosevelt brought the two sides to Portsmouth, New Hampshire, where a treaty was signed in September 1905 ending the war. For the first time in modern history an Asian nation had defeated a European in a war. The treaty recognized Japan's influence in Korea and southern Manchuria and propelled Japan to the forefront of Pacific powers.

Meanwhile, while Japan was flexing her muscles in the western Pacific, the anti-Japanese movement in California picked up steam. The *San Francisco Chronicle* began a major anti-Japanese campaign in 1905,[30] and anti-Japanese editorials appeared throughout the Monterey Bay Region.

SAN FRANCISCO SCHOOL BOARD CRISIS

Following the destructive earthquake of April 1906 (Japan sent a considerable sum of money as aid to the people of San Francisco), the San Francisco school board decided to segregate all Asian immigrant children into a separate Oriental School. President Roosevelt knew how powerful Japan was, and fearful that the Japanese government would take offense to the San Francisco school board's action, he invited the school board to Washington, D.C. Roosevelt assured the school board that he would do what he could to limit Japanese immigration if the board would rescind its action. The school board agreed, and Roosevelt began a delicate negotiation with Japan to further limit immigration to the United States.

GENTLEMAN'S AGREEMENT: 1907-8

In 1907 in a diplomatic note known as the Gentleman's Agreement, the Japanese government agreed to stop issuing new passports to Japanese laborers. Japan further agreed to allow the United States to prohibit the movement of Japanese nationals from Hawaii to California (which Roosevelt did by executive order).

The agreement effectively ended the emigration of Japanese laborers to California from both Japan and Hawaii. Scholars, merchants, and students could continue to come to the United States from Japan. Most importantly, the agreement permitted the wives of Japanese men already in California to receive passports and emigrate. This agreement had profound impact on the nature of the Japanese community in the United States and the Monterey Bay Region. Though the number of Japanese immigrants to the United States dropped after 1907, it consisted mostly of women, changing the Japanese community from one of single men to one of families. And the children of these marriages who were born in the United States were United States citizens.

SUMMARY

The period 1887 to 1907 was dominated by the Issei finding and developing their economic niches in the region. By 1907 they were major players both in agriculture and fishing. But no matter how American they became, the forces of racism and prejudice followed. After the change in immigration pattern in 1907, they settled in and tried to consolidate and preserve what they had achieved.

4 ERA OF THE FIRST FAMILIES
1907 TO 1925

With their immigration limited almost exclusively to wives and family members, the Japanese began to concentrate on putting down permanent roots and making the region their home. During this period, from 1907 to 1925, they not only developed new economic niches in agriculture and commercial fishing in the region but continued to replace the aging Chinese in wood-chopping and railroad work.

The Japantowns throughout the region grew and matured, and the Japanese continued to reject the completely segregated roll that the Chinese had taken in the nineteenth century.

The people of California responded to these circumstances by trying to drive the Japanese out of the agricultural industry. Two alien land laws (1913 and 1920) were clear statements of the will of the majority of Californians. Despite the laws, however, the Japanese continued to be major players in the region's agriculture into the 1920s.

The Japanese also found that statements and acts of loyalty towards the United States during World War I counted for little when the final push toward Japanese exclusion appeared in the early 1920s. The low point for the Issei came when immigration from Japan was outlawed by the United States government in 1924.

Yet, despite the narrowing of their world, the Issei continued to work towards making a permanent home in the Monterey Bay Region.

Prospective brides sent photographs such as this one to their intended husbands in the United States. The men sent similar formal photographs of themselves to Japan.   YAMAGUCHI FAMILY

JAPANESE WOMEN ARRIVE

By all accounts, the Japanese government carefully adhered to its immigration agreements with the United States. Thus, as required by the Gentleman's Agreement, in 1908 the Japanese government stopped issuing new passports to Japanese laborers, allowing only three groups to emigrate to the United States after that date: 1) former residents; 2) parents, wives, or children of residents; and 3) settled

Most Japanese-American family albums contain photographs of Issei picture brides such as this.   GOTA FAMILY

agriculturists.[1] The effect of the Gentleman's Agreement was a remarkable increase in the number of Japanese women and families in the region. (See chart on p. 46)

PICTURE BRIDES

As many of the Issei men entered their second decade in the region, they began to think about marriage. Local newspapers occasionally reported the return of a local Japanese with a new bride, but most Issei could afford neither the money nor the time to travel back to Japan to get a wife. By 1910 the most common method of marriage was to have the families in Japan arrange a wedding by proxy and then send the woman to the United States to meet her new husband.

The requirements for these proxy marriages were quite stringent and, like everything else about Japanese immigration, carefully monitored by the Japanese government. In the early years of the Gentleman's Agreement, only Issei who were businessmen with at least $1,000 in capital qualified for the process. In 1915 the Japanese government relaxed the requirement and allowed even laborers to bring wives to the United States, though they had to have $800 in cash to qualify.[2]

The women in these arranged marriages were often called *omiai,* or "photo brides," because the exchange of photographs was the only way the couple saw each other before the woman's arrival in California. This relatively impersonal way of marrying probably seems odd in the 1990s, but it was not uncommon for European immigrant men to matchmake through photographs and family representatives after they came to the United States. The only difference in the case of the Japanese was the actual wedding ceremony in Japan, where the groom had a family stand-in. The wedding was an essential part of the picture bride system because the couple had to be married before the Japanese government would issue the woman a passport.

This picture-bride process fell very much in line with traditional Japanese marriage practices, wherein the families made the decisions and the entire event was negotiated using go-betweens. Traditional Japanese marriages were for the benefit of the families, not the couple. Love was not considered a sound foundation for such an important institution in Japanese society.[3] (Even today in Japan, it is estimated that upwards of 40% of marriages are arranged with go-betweens.)

Once the bride arrived in America, however, the pressures on her were way beyond what she would have endured in Japan. First, many of the men exaggerated their status in the United States. They may have met the qualifications of businessman on paper, but the reality was a small boardinghouse or labor camp stuck in the middle of nowhere. Then there was the reality of their new husband versus the idealization of him back in Japan. Already ten to fifteen years older than the women, the men sometimes substituted photographs of themselves looking much younger than they actually were. Once here, the wives usually assumed the double burden of not only taking care of the household but also working in the field beside their new husband.

The shock that these women felt when hit with the reality of life in the United States must have been enormous: dressed in new American clothing, not speaking the language, meeting a husband who may have misrepresented himself, and moving to a house which did not fit the idealized vision seen in Japan. Yuki Torigoe remembered coming to Watsonville:

I came to the United States happily since I had heard that the United States was a good country. [Laughter.] I had some kind of idea about the United States since I had seen many pictures. I believed that all the houses were grandly made out of blocks and concrete. But when I came to my own house in the United States, it was made out of wood. I thought that could not be.[4]

It is a testimony to the strength (and often pressures) of the Japanese communities in the region that most of these marriages worked as well as they did. The lives of the Issei women were mostly about sacrifice and hard work, and the annals of the older Japanese families are filled with stories of persevering in the face of incredible odds.

TRAGEDY AND DEATH

There is another, darker side to this story, rarely mentioned by historians from within the Japanese communities. Not everyone was able to adjust. The early years are sprinkled with

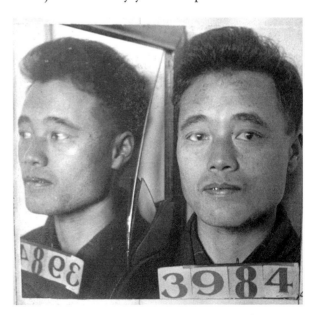

Tiaji Kamigaka murdered his wife in Watsonville in 1918 and was sentenced to life in San Quentin prison.[5]   SPECIAL COLLECTIONS, UCSC

stories of desertions, suicides, murders, and murder-suicides, all of which amplify just how difficult those early years must have been.

For example, there was the tragic story of a picture bride in Watsonville who made the acquaintance of another Japanese man, fell in love, and committed a few "indiscretions." The shame of her activities caused the couple to move to a lonely labor camp in the Salinas Valley, where the onus of what she had done finally drove the woman to commit suicide.[6]

Sometimes the loneliness and culture shock were just too much to bear. A twenty-year-old Japanese woman living on a ranch north of Watsonville grew so despondent about her prospects in America that she came home from Japanese School one afternoon and committed suicide by swallowing a huge dose of strychnine. Her friends said that she was homesick for her relatives back in Japan and, with no money for the return trip, decided to end her life.[7]

Suicide was not confined to Issei women. Several Japanese men killed themselves during these early years, including a young man working in a logging camp in the Aptos Canyon in 1919. His failure to return to his cabin prompted a search which ended when his body was found hanging from a tree. He, too, had been despondent and had threatened to take his own life.[8]

Most studies of Japanese crime in the United States during the early twentieth century have emphasized the extremely low number of violent crimes committed by Japanese immigrants. When compared to the general American population, Japanese immigrants had an exceptionally low crime rate in proportion to their numbers.[9] However, within the very small numbers there is an element of violence, suggesting an incredible price paid by the Issei as they attempted to shape their future in an extremely hostile American landscape.

PICTURE BRIDE PRACTICE ENDS

Believing that President Roosevelt had stopped all Japanese immigration during the 1907-8 negotiations (the agreement was kept a secret), the anti-Japanese forces in California felt betrayed by the coming of the photo brides.

Following the temporary suspension of the anti-Japanese movement during World War I (see further on in this chapter), increasing pressure was brought to stop the immigration of Japanese women. Always sensitive to their international reputation, the Japanese government stopped issuing passports to women in the spring of 1920. In striking contrast to all other Asian immigrant groups prior to the 1960s, the Japanese community in California was one of wives and families.

THE NUMBERS TELL THE STORY: 1900-1920

During the 20 years from 1900-1920, over 33% of the Japanese community became U.S. citizens by virtue of their birth. The median age of the 1,116 Nisei in the 1920 census was 5.0 years. The combined effect of Chinese Exclusion and the Gentleman's Agreement can be seen when comparing the profile of the Chinese living in the Monterey Bay region in 1920 with that of the Japanese. Not only was the Chinese community only ⅓ the size but females comprised only 16% of the Chinese community. The median age of the 266 America-born Chinese in the region was 17 years.

Year	Total Japanese	U.S. Born	%	Women	%
1900	960	4	.4%	20	2%
1910	2,096	253	12%	454	22%
1920	3,060	1,116	36%	1,266	41%
	Total Chinese				
1920	1,051	266	25%	162	16%

(The numbers are the totals of Monterey, Santa Cruz, and San Benito Counties, derived from the manuscript federal census schedules of each county.)

JAPANESE ASSOCIATIONS

Japanese associations were the primary Issei organizations in the Monterey Bay Region. From their establishment around 1910 until 1920, when the photo-bride practice was stopped by the Japanese government, the associations oversaw the process by which most Issei men married women back in Japan. The associations also provided the social core for the Japanese communities by staging cultural events and picnics throughout the year. Their most important role was as intermediaries between the Japanese immigrant communities and the larger communities within which they lived. These associations were mini-consulates, providing important legal and technical information as well as conveying the advice of the Japanese government. And for the non-Japanese community, the associations were the official voice of the Japanese community.

In many ways the Japanese associations were similar to benevolent associations formed by other immigrants groups, such as the Chinese, Jews, or the Italians, which cared for the sick and buried the dead. The added element of international politics made the Japanese associations a little more "official" than the others.

SALINAS JAPANESE ASSOCIATION

Founded in 1905, the Salinas Japanese Association provided leadership and counsel to the early Japanese community in the Salinas Valley. One of the initial concerns of the community was the lack of a suitable cemetery. During the early years, Japanese burials took place in the public cemetery near the county hospital on the north side of Salinas, adjacent to the Chinese cemetery. In 1908 the association purchased a two-acre site for a cemetery on Abbott Street in the south part of town and started a cemetery named the Yamato Cemetery. All of the Japanese previously buried out at the county hospital were then moved to the new site in 1911.[10]

WATSONVILLE JAPANESE ASSOCIATION

Founded in 1910, the Watsonville Japanese Association played not only an administrative and official role in the community but also a social one. The primary social event for all the regional Japanese communities was their annual picnics. The Watsonville Japanese Association also sponsored floats in July Fourth parades and booked many traveling cultural shows for the community, song and dance groups in the early years and films from Japan in later years. The association also organized Japanese language schools for the new generation of Nisei.

Asami Family, Pajaro Valley, c. 1920. The close spacing of children in the early families is apparent in this photograph. The children were all American citizens by birth.

MRS. WALTER HASHIMOTO

But perhaps the most important and visible role was as the go-between with the greater community in which they lived. As the anti-Japanese movement gained steam, the Watsonville Japanese Association held frequent public meetings featuring speakers from the San Francisco Bay Area to help explain the issues.

MONTEREY JAPANESE ASSOCIATION

The first mention of such an organization occurs in 1908, when the Monterey Japanese Association donated $100 towards the celebration of the visit of the Great White Fleet in Monterey. The influence of the association in Monterey seems to have been somewhat muted by the Japanese Fishermen's Union, which often acted as the go-between with the larger community in Monterey. Eventually, the association built a hall on Adams Street in 1926.[11]

SANTA CRUZ JAPANESE ASSOCIATION

Even though Santa Cruz had the smallest number of Japanese residents in the region, there was a Japanese association hall in the Farmer's Union building in downtown Santa Cruz. The first mention of the organization came in a 1910 newspaper account of the celebration of Emperor Meiji's birthday on November 3.[12] The organization was led by laundry owner Masaya Tan, the most prominent Japanese in the city. Tan owned a laundry on Bulkhead Street.

CHURCHES, TEMPLES, AND ADAPTATION

For most immigrants in America, churches, synagogues, and temples were the linchpins of their communities. The Japanese were no exception, and very early following their arrival in the Monterey Bay Region, Christian churches and Buddhist temples arose within the various communities. The emergence of these institutions is more remarkable in the case of the Japanese, however, because religion was not a central part of Tokugawa culture, nor is it a major element in Japanese society even today.

The culture of Tokugawa Japan was a secular one. The number of temples and shrines all over Japan from that era gives the impression that the Japanese are a deeply religious people, but this should be seen as yet another example of the Japanese reluctance to discard. The buildings may be there and the Japanese may participate in religious festivals

Japanese community float, Monterey, c. 1910. The Japanese associations usually sponsored Japanese parade entries throughout the region. The American flag was often a major element of the float.   GOTA FAMILY

throughout the year, but they do not see themselves as religious. Religion was (and is) much more about belonging to a group than about faith. Using the Judeo-Christian measures of commitment and dedication, the Japanese who came to the United States were not religious.

As noted in Chapter 2, Christianity

Watsonville Buddhist Temple, 1919. Funeral for Mrs. Natsu Tao. This wonderful traditional Japanese building stood on Union Street until it was torn down in 1964.   BILL TAO

was driven out of Japan by the Tokugawa shogun in the seventeenth century. The ban was lifted in 1873 as part of the Meiji reforms, but Christianity never claimed more than 2% of the Japanese population as members, a proportion that continues to this day.[13]

Then how is it that Christian churches came to be so important in the Japanese communities in the United States and the Monterey Bay Region? Again the answer lies in the ability of the Issei to adapt. The Japanese immigrants saw

that religious institutions were an important part of the American landscape, so they made them an important part of their own. As added inducements, the Christian churches conducted English-language classes for the Issei immigrants and in some instances even provided short-term room and board.[14]

It is not surprising, therefore, that the Christian churches in the region predate the Buddhist temples by almost a decade.

JAPANESE CHRISTIAN CHURCHES WITH FOUNDING DATES

Watsonville Presbyterian Mission - 1898
Present Name: Westview Presbyterian Church
Address: 118 First Street
Watsonville

Salinas Presbyterian Mission - 1898
Present Name: Lincoln Avenue Presbyterian Church
Address: 536 Lincoln Avenue
Salinas

Monterey Peninsula Presbyterian Mission - 1908
Present Name: El Estero Presbyterian Church
Address: Pearl Street and Camino El Estero
Monterey

Westview Presbyterian Church, Watsonville, 1996.   SANDY LYDON

THE REGION'S BUDDHIST TEMPLES

The first Buddhist temple in California was established in San Francisco in 1899.[15] The Monterey Bay Region's first Buddhist temple was organized in Watsonville in 1905 by the heads of several Japanese labor clubs. The group met in the Watsonville Opera House until the first Buddhist temple was completed on Union Street. Some of the funds for the new temple were raised from a group of interested non-Japanese in Santa Cruz.[16]

The Issei then applied their adaptive powers to Japanese Buddhism, and over time the traditional Buddhist core was surrounded by some very Judeo-Christian forms. Buddhist congregations held services on Sundays and built pews in the temples, practices not found in Japan. Even the song "Buddha Loves Me, This I Know" and other hymns found their way into regular use. However, as Santa Cruz County Sansei Kim Sakamoto points out, these adaptations provide an "appearance of safety on the outside to protect the integrity of practice on the inside."[17]

One by-product of traditional Japanese attitudes towards organized religion was a strong sense of religious toleration. In each of the three Monterey Bay Region communities, Japanese, Christians, and Buddhists lived comfortably side by side. When pressed in interviews, however, all longtime Japanese residents recall very spirited competitions that broke along religious lines. This was particularly true in the Japanese intramural athletic leagues, where the Christian church usually sponsored a team, the Buddhist temple another. These rivalries rarely extended beyond the end of the game or match, however.

JAPANESE EMPLOYMENT IN THE REGION: OLD NICHES

The Japanese involvement in the region's economy was solidified between the years 1907 and 1925, and agriculture was the primary focus of Issei energy. However, there were several other areas in which the Japanese made major contributions, and these have been divided into two

BUDDHIST TEMPLES WITH FOUNDING DATES

Watsonville Buddhist Temple - 1906
Present Name: Watsonville Buddhist Temple
Address: 423 Bridge Street
Watsonville

Salinas Buddhist Temple - 1925
Present Name: Buddhist Temple of Salinas
Address: 14 California Street
Salinas

Monterey Buddhist Temple - 1956
Present Name: Monterey Peninsula Buddhist Temple
Address: 1155 Noche Buena Street
Seaside

Watsonville Buddhist Temple, Riverside Drive. This modern building was completed and dedicated in 1956.   SANDY LYDON

categories: old niches, or those occupations where the Chinese and early Japanese immigrants were already established, and new niches, which the Japanese developed from the ground up.

WORKING ON THE RAILROADS

By 1900 most of the major railroad lines in the region had already been built with the Chinese providing almost all the labor. There are fleeting references to Japanese laborers working on the northern end of the Ocean Shore Railroad just outside San Francisco in 1907,[18] but the logging railroads and other short lines built after 1900 all seem to have been built by non-Asian laborers.

Japanese laborers were used extensively along the Pacific coast as railroad section hands, helping to clear track and maintain the railroad beds. Professor Yuji Ichioka has documented the wide use of Japanese on the Northern Pacific Railroad, for example, and to a lesser extent their use by the Southern Pacific in California.

Japanese laborers were used extensively to maintain existing rail lines in the Monterey Bay Region. In 1904 S.P. apparently fired some Italian section hands, replacing them with Japanese. The following evening one of the Italians blew up the shack the Japanese were sleeping in just outside Monterey, injuring several of the new Japanese railroad hands.[19] In 1907 several dozen Japanese section hands were clearing track near Felton.[20]

FIREWOOD BUSINESS

Chinese woodcutters had been working in the Monterey Bay Region since the 1870s, cutting firewood as part of reclamation leases negotiated with landowners in the Pajaro and Salinas Valleys.[21] From their earliest arrival in the region, the Japanese were involved in the firewood cutting business. Land clearing and the firewood business went hand in hand, with the firewood a valuable by-product of the cutting. The David Jacks records at the Huntington Library in San Marino contain a number of wood cutting agreements between Jacks and Monterey labor contractor Onojiro Uchida. The following 1910 agreement is worth quoting at length, as it gives us an insight into the technology of firewood cutting:

> Uchida is to cut three hundred cords of pine wood for said corporation of which fifty cords are to be 12" long, 150 cords to be 14" long and the remaining 100 to be 16" long all to be cut in even and uniform lengths and to be well piled between stakes which are to be well driven into the ground, placed 8 feet apart and wired together near the top end to prevent spreading, and each pile of wood is to be four feet and three inches high, and two such piles or tiers are to be called one cord . . . . All the sound down timber that is over four inches in diameter is to be cut into wood first before cutting any standing timber, and no rotten or otherwise imperfect woods are to be piled, nor any rough or knotty pieces are to be placed into the piles of wood . . . . [Jacks] Corporation shall furnish Inspector when wood is piled and no piling is to be done when inspector is not present.

Uchida had three months to fulfill the contract and the Jacks Corporation agreed to pay him $1.50 per cord.[22] Uchida must have fulfilled his end of such bargains, as there are at least a dozen of such agreements in the Jacks Collection.

Japanese woodcutters were also very much involved in the regional tanbark industry. (Local tanneries used the bark of the tan oak tree as a source of tannin, the primary chemical used in processing hides into leather.)

A NEW NICHE: SPLIT STUFF

The Monterey Bay Region's redwood lumber industry was almost entirely closed to Asian immigrants. Chinese were allowed to build the logging railroads in the mountains and act as logging camp cooks, but they did not participate in the falling, transporting, or milling of redwood lumber. Chinese woodcutting crews sometimes worked under contract in the woods to cut firewood, but there are no recorded instances in the region where Chinese were directly involved in logging.

The Japanese found the logging industry closed in the 1890s, not only because of a prejudice against Asian laborers in the woods, but also because the industry was in the throes of a major depression and many regional mills had either cut employment or closed altogether.

Japanese split stuff camp, Aptos canyon c. 1915. Split posts and pickets can be seen piled up the mountain behind the camp.   STOODLEY COLLECTION

When the depression passed, however, the Japanese were able to enter the woods and work in a very specialized niche, the manufacture of what is known as "split stuff."

A good part of the manufactured redwood that came out of the region's forests did not go through a lumber mill but was actually split on site into shakes, pickets, posts, and railroad ties. The grapestakes, which literally held up California's wine industry, were but one of many products of the split lumber industry. The split lumber was then transported to railroad landings on the backs of mules.

Since the manufacture of split lumber was seen as a notch below that of milled lumber in the hierarchy of the redwood forests, when the economy was strong enough to offer full employment to all available Caucasian loggers, the Japanese were allowed to negotiate split stuff contracts. Several regional lumber producers, including Santa Cruz's Frederick Augustus Hihn, had crews of Japanese working in the forests during the first two decades of the twentieth century.

A good example of Japanese split stuff logging occurred in the Aptos Canyon between 1910 and 1918, when a large crew of Japanese men cut over ten million board feet of split stuff for the Molino Timber Company. One of the company's owners later remembered his surprise at seeing the huge sacks of rice and barrels of *shoyu* (soy sauce) that went into the lumber camp. He also noted that the first structure that the Japanese built was their *ofuro,* or Japanese-style bathtub.

The autonomy and independence of working in their own logging camp no doubt was attractive to the Japanese, as was their being paid by the quantity and quality of their work, rather than a daily wage.[23]

The only legacy of the Japanese woodcutters is the name "Jap Camp," on the west flank of China Ridge in the present-day Forest of Nisene Marks State Park. The site was occupied by the Japanese loggers for several years, but today there are no buildings, signs, or other indications that the Japanese were ever there.

A New Niche: Japanese Commercial Salmon Fishermen

Japanese immigrants played an integral role in the origins of the fish canning business which eventually became the economic mainstay of Monterey. The first successful canning operation in the region was a small cannery built by two abalone cannery owners from Oakland. Joseph and Edward Gayetty (they were brothers) began canning abalone in May of 1900. Their cannery was perched on a ledge above a small beach about a mile and a half south of Point Lobos, and all the abalone canned there were caught by Japanese divers living at Point Lobos.

The Gayetty cannery operated steadily into early 1902 when the brothers closed it, selling the equipment to a cannery on the San Luis Obispo County coast at Cayucos. The precedent had been set. The Gayettys proved that the canning of abalone and other sea products could be profitable on the Monterey Peninsula.

The same year that the Gayettys closed their abalone cannery, Otosaburo Noda and Henry

Gayetty Abalone Cannery, Wildcat Canyon, c. 1901. Japanese divers furnished all the abalone for this first successful canning operation in the Monterey Area.

Malpas formed the Monterey Fishing and Canning Company to can both abalone and salmon. The Monterey sardine canning industry, later made famous by John Steinbeck in his novel *Cannery Row*, actually began around the canning of salmon and abalone at the turn of the century.[24]

Though the word "canning" was used in the process, the salmon were actually smoked or cured and then packed in a brine solution in barrels for shipment. Salmon were not put in metal cans in Monterey until 1911.[25]

JAPANESE SALMON FISHERMEN

The salmon that went into these packing houses were caught in small sailing skiffs with hook and line. Of the twenty-five or so small boats supplying the canneries during the first year, only ten were sailed by Japanese fishermen. As the number of canneries increased during that first decade, so did the number of fishing boats, the preponderant number being owned and operated by Japanese fishermen. By 1907, 125 of Monterey's 180 salmon boats were Japanese.[26] During the first decade of salmon packing, the Japanese comprised approximately 70% of the Monterey salmon fishing fleet.

Japanese fishing boats at anchor, Monterey, c. 1910. The Japanese fishermen trolled for salmon in small sail-powered boats.
MONTEREY PUBLIC LIBRARY

In 1904 a union of Japanese and non-Japanese fishermen staged a brief stoppage at the beginning of the canning season in order to get a higher per pound rate for their fish. By 1907 the Japanese were organized together in the Japanese Fishermen's Union, while the non-Japanese fishermen had their own union.

In 1906, Frank Booth, president of the Sacramento River Packers Association, invited Sicilian fishermen to move from the company's headquarters in Pittsburgh, California, to Monterey. Most historians suggest that Pietro Ferrante, the leader of the Sicilian fishermen, was encouraged by Booth to come to Monterey to focus on the sardine industry, but it also may have been an effort to break the hold that Japanese fishermen were gaining over the salmon fishing industry.

SALMON SEASON

The Japanese salmon fishermen pursued their catch primarily in small, one-man, sail-powered skiffs. Even with the vagaries of the migrating salmon and contract prices, a Japanese fisherman could earn up to $25 per day at the peak of the salmon season. Compared to the $2 per day which Japanese farm laborers earned during those years, salmon fishing was a very lucrative occupation.

The official salmon canning season usually lasted from May 15 to August 15, but the salmon sometimes began appearing in the bay as early as March 1. Later contracts were written so that Japanese fishermen wishing to catch salmon before the "official" season could do so and sell them to the canners who then shipped

JAPANESE SEASONS OF WORK: c.1914			
March 1	August 1	December 1	March 15
Salmon Season	Fruit Harvest and Fruit Drying	Woodcutting Land Clearing	

them as fresh fish to San Francisco. The fishing boats were stored in boatyards during the winter, and usually by the first of April of each year, most of the Japanese boats had been refurbished and put back into the water for the season. When the salmon finally departed the bay in early fall, the Japanese put their boats back in storage.

During the fishing off-season, the Japanese salmon fishermen worked as laborers on nearby farms or in local forests, clearing brush and cutting firewood.

MONTEREY SARDINE INDUSTRY

The sardine canning industry developed alongside the salmon packers at Monterey. One reason for this was the complementary seasons, because the sardines usually appeared as salmon season was winding down in August and lasted until mid-February of the following year. Eventually, between salmon and sardines, the Monterey canners experimented with various types of canning and packing so that they could work year round.

Where salmon were caught with hook and line, the much smaller sardines were caught with nets. Almost from the outset, the catching of the small fish was in the hands of the Sicilian immigrant fishermen, many of whom had come down from Pittsburgh in 1906. The Sicilians used gill nets in the early years to snag the small fish, but Ferrante is credited with introducing an old-country net called a "lampara." By the beginning of World War I, the lampara net was providing the bulk of the sardine catch for Monterey's canneries, and the Sicilians dominated that industry.

WORLD WAR I

The beginning of world war in Europe in 1914 had an almost immediate effect on the Monterey salmon fishing industry. The bulk of the cured salmon had been shipped to Germany, and with that market now in disarray, the price of salmon began to fall. By 1917 a local newspaper declared the German salmon market "totally closed."[27]

Monterey Fishermen's Wharf. Sicilian fishermen eventually came to dominate the sardine fishing industry at Monterey.   PAT HATHAWAY

The war's effect on the sardine industry was exactly the opposite: orders for the canned fish poured in from both civilian and military buyers.

The effect of the shift from salmon to sardines in the Monterey fishing industry had a predictable effect on the Japanese fishermen. A tally made by the California Division of Fish and Game over the 1920-21 and 1921-22 canning seasons concluded that 86% of the fishermen men were either Italian or Americans of Italian ancestry (most of them were Sicilians), while 10% were Japanese, 3% Spanish, with the remaining 1% a mixture of ethnicities. (It is interesting to note that none of the sardine fishermen was Chinese.)[28]

In the 1920s the Japanese added a half-ring to the bottom of the lampara, which increased the sizes of their catch, and the Sicilians quickly followed suit. But when the huge purse seiners came into the industry in 1926, only a few Japanese fishermen were able to take the next step. By the late 1930s there were only a dozen or so Japanese sardine fishermen working out of Monterey. As we shall see, World War II ended the half-century of involvement of the Japanese in the fishing industry of Monterey Bay.

AGRICULTURE: FROM LABORERS TO LANDOWNERS

Agriculture was the primary occupational niche for the Japanese in California and the Monterey Bay Region. Beginning with their arrival as seasonal laborers in the 1890s through their evolution to landowners, the Japanese provided the motive power and muscle that turned the wheels of the region's agricultural engine into the 1920s. Their being both Japanese and successful brought the full force of discriminatory legislation upon them.

FIGHT OVER THE LAND

Landownership was never an issue in the anti-Chinese movement in the Monterey Bay Region. The Chinese were unable to amass enough money or feel a strong enough sense of security to purchase property. With the exception of parts of Castroville's Chinatown in the 1890s, the Chinese did not purchase land here.

The Japanese, on the other hand, moved quickly from farm laborers to leaseholders to landowners. Many historians have used this difference in landownership pat-

Japanese apple pickers, Pajaro Valley, c. 1910. Japanese worked in a number of migratory farm labor capacities, including picking apples.

BILL TAO

tern as evidence of a "sojourner attitude" on the part of the Chinese, but this is much too simplistic. A partial list of the causes should include:

1. Presence of Japanese families compared to absence of Chinese. The entire Japanese immigrant/adaptation process was accelerated by the early presence of Japanese families. Investment in property is a natural outgrowth of families planning for the future.
2. Japanese willingness to pool resources in non-family businesses. Chinese businessmen were reluctant to go beyond family members when forming businesses, making it difficult for them to amass enough capital to buy land.
3. Japanese more adaptive. Though this point should not be pushed too far, it is clear that Japanese immigrants learned the rules and adapted to them much more quickly than their Chinese counterparts.
4. More small land parcels available in 1910 than 1860. When the Chinese first arrived in the region, many of the huge Mexican land grants were still intact. Fifty year's worth of subdivision created many smaller, affordable parcels of land.
5. Overall greater sense of security within the Japanese community. Even though the anti-Japanese rhetoric began immediately upon their arrival, the Japanese were much more organized than the Chinese. And, with a powerful homeland to speak for them, the Japanese no doubt felt much more comfortable in the region than the Chinese had in the nineteenth century.

As the Japanese began to buy farmland, the anti-Japanese forces turned up the volume. At the core of all this, of course, was that the Japanese had forgotten their PLACE. They had moved from employees to competitors and good ones at that. As the editor of a Monterey newspaper observed in 1908, "[The Japanese] are acquiring control of the land and its products as well."[29]

Shinyu Labor Club, Watsonville, c. 1910. Labor clubs such as this one were the primary contractors for Japanese farm laborers during the early years.   BILL TAO

STAGE #1 - MIGRATORY FARM LABOR

Throughout the period 1907 to 1925, the majority of Japanese continued to work for daily wages in the region's fields. They worked in the sugar beet fields, orchards, potato fields, vegetable fields, and berry patches throughout the region. The majority of them were migratory, moving within and beyond the region as the seasons changed. As the *Watsonville Pajaronian* observed in 1916, "Japanese laborers travel from one place to another somewhat like the fruit tramps that come to this valley and leave at the end of apple season."[30] And their importance to industries such as the growing of sugar beets was simply stated by the *Monterey Cypress* in 1910, when they observed that if the Japanese were to leave the fields "not a sugar beet would be planted or harvested thereafter."[31] The general wage during this period was two dollar per day plus board.

STAGE #2 - SHARECROPPER

Once a laborer or group of laborers had built up enough capital they entered into agreements with landowners from whom they received a percentage of the profit at season's end. The split was often fifty-fifty, but the percentages could vary depending on what was provided by the landowner. If the landowner put up equipment and seed along with the land, he might take a bigger slice of the season's profits. For the Japanese, however, these arrangements were much more desirable than working on a day/wage basis through the labor club. Since the returns were tied directly to their effort, harder work usually paid off in more money at the end of the season.

The David Jacks papers at the Huntington Library in San Marino provide many early examples of sharecropping leases. In November 1906, Otosaburo Noda and S. Nao entered into a three-year fifty-fifty split on the property in Saucito Canyon known as the pear orchard. Jacks provided the land and the orchard, and for their part the Japanese agreed to keep up the land, cut fallen trees into firewood, and "poison the squirrels, gophers and moles," as well as harvest the fruit and deliver it to downtown Monterey.[32]

STAGE #3 - LEASEHOLDER

Outright land leases were even better than sharecropping; if the Issei provided all the necessary equipment and labor, they received all the profits once the cost of the lease was paid. Some of the leases involved land already in production, but some were reclamation leases, where the Japanese agreed to clear and bring the land into production in exchange for free use of the land for five years. The reclamation lease had been a major part of Chinese agriculture in the region in the 1880s and 1890s, and both they and the Japanese agreed that it usually took four years to bring marginal willow or tule land into

Strawberries being loaded onto the train, Watsonville, c. 1922. Kumajiro Murakami, left, was one of many Japanese farmers who were influential in the strawberry industry.   BILL TAO

production. Usually it was the last year's profit that made or broke the arrangement. The downside of leaseholding was that the landowners often required a cash payment up front, and not all Japanese were able to scrape up enough money to do this.

It was just a decade after Sakuzo Kimura's 1892 arrival in the Pajaro Valley that the first lease between a Japanese farmer and white landowner was recorded in Santa Cruz County. In June of 1902, S. J. Duckworth leased thirty acres of land beside Corralitos Creek to S. Madokoro at $600 per year to grow strawberries. The Duckworths also leased adjacent land to T. Higashi for an annual rent of $800 for the same purpose. The following years saw an increasing number of similar transactions, as the Japanese pooled their resources to work for themselves rather than as laborers.

By 1908 a Monterey newspaper noted that Japanese berry companies were "taking long leases on berry lands of the Pajaro Valley." The editor lamented that where once the Japanese were the laborers they now were "acquiring control of the land and its products as well."[33] The leasing of land by Japanese was still newsworthy enough in 1909 for the Watsonville newspaper to note the signing of a lease between the Kobayashi brothers and M. T. Rose. The Kobayashis leased a seventy-acre apple orchard from Rose for a period of five years for an annual rent of $2,200.[34] In 1910 Japanese farmers negotiated a two year lease in the Carmel Valley to raise potatoes and vegetables, paying $40/acre per year. This was the highest price paid up to that time to rent agricultural land in the region.[35]

STAGE #4 - LANDOWNER

Under the most ideal conditions, once a Japanese farmer was successful enough to amass the required capital, the outright purchase of farmland was the next step. Unfortunately, non-Japanese farmers and politicians became enraged when the Japanese began to purchase farmland. It was one thing when a farm laborer was industriously working FOR the farmer and quite another when he was using that same industry in competition AGAINST him.

Japanese farmer, Carmel Valley, c. 1915. Several Japanese farmers worked the bottom land near the old San Carlos Mission in Carmel Valley.   MIYAMOTO FAMILY

THE FIRST ALIEN LAND LAW - 1913

Following the success by anti-Japanese interests in California to limit Japanese immigration in 1908 (they believed, erroneously, that they had ended it), several California legislators began a campaign to limit the lives and businesses of Japanese already here.[36] Numerous bills were introduced in the California legislature in 1909, and Federal officials, ever-mindful of the growing military power of Japan, continued their efforts to reign in the impetuous Californians.

THE REGIONAL ANTI-JAPANESE MOVEMENT 1909 - 1913

There had been sporadic outbursts of anti-Japanese sentiment expressed in the region since the mid-1890s. The most virulent and success-

A PRO-JAPANESE OASIS

Pro-Japanese immigration supporter. One of the region's most outspoken critics of the efforts to restrict Japanese immigration was William T. Sesnon, pictured here sitting (left) on the porch of his Soquel summer home with fellow directors of the Panama-Pacific International Exposition and their wives, 1915.

The Sesnon summer home, Soquel. Though the main house had no elements of Japanese architecture, the grounds and interior were heavily influenced by Japanese art.

Shinto gate on grounds of Sesnon home. The gardens around the Sesnon home were designed by John McClaren, who also designed San Francisco's Golden Gate Park. The grounds had a very strong Japanese theme, including this traditional Shinto gate, along with extensive plantings of bamboo.

Interior of Sesnon's home at Soquel. Sesnon combined his strong feelings about Japanese immigration with a love of Japanese art. The interior of his Soquel summer home included a large Japanese Buddha seated in an alcove off the living room.

SESNON FAMILY

ful of these had centered around limiting the Japanese abalone divers working along the Monterey Peninsula shoreline. In September 1909, in concert with the anti-Japanese chorus in Sacramento, a series of meetings was held in Salinas sponsored by the Monterey County Chamber of Commerce to organize an anti-Japanese movement in the Monterey Bay Region.

At a banquet held at the Hotel Abbott on September 25, 1909, some forty regional business leaders declared unanimous opposition to "this yellow tidal wave of coolie labor that is sweeping over the Pacific."[37] The use of language harking back to the successful anti-Chinese movement of the 1870s was certainly not accidental, but the meeting seemed to mix its metaphors, freely interchanging "yellow" and "little brown men" during the evening. For those with long enough memories, the theme was exactly the same as the one that had been raised against the Chinese—they, the Japanese, must be replaced in the fields. The old warmed-over litanies included the complaint that the Japanese were sending all their money back to Japan and that their being in the fields was driving out good, hard working white folks who might wish to find employment.

SHOWDOWN IN SACRAMENTO, 1913

Meanwhile, the anti-Japanese forces in California kept the pressure on throughout the period 1910-1912, while the federal government continued to cajole and wheedle the legislature into not provoking Japan by doing something stupid. The whole thing came to a head in early 1913, when several alien land laws were introduced into the California legislature. President Woodrow Wilson vowed to keep California in check, and California's Progressive Republican governor watched the anti-Japanese bills grind

their way through the legislative process.

The alien land law was relatively straightforward—it would prohibit the ownership of property in California to anyone "ineligible to American citizenship" and limit leases to such people to three years or less. The indirectness of the language—the words "Japanese" or "Japan" were not in the bill—was not lost on the bill's opponents. Nor was the way to circumvent the law—put the land in the names of the ever growing group of Nisei who were citizens by birth.

The Alien Land Law passed 35 to 2 in the State Senate and 72 to 3 in the Assembly, and it was signed by Governor Hiram Johnson on May 19, 1913.

RESPONSE OF THE JAPANESE COMMUNITIES

The Japanese in California did not sit idly by during the alien land law debate. They lobbied and held meetings to discuss strategies, and once the bill was signed into law, discussions were held throughout California about mounting a boycott against the legislators who had voted for the bill. (They would have had to boycott just about everyone, of course.) On May 23 there was a huge meeting of the Japanese community in Watsonville, and representatives from both the Japanese government and the California Japanese associations explained the new law and counseled the local Japanese to be "conservative and good citizens."[38] Similar meetings were held in Japanese communities elsewhere in the region, and eventually, the emotions subsided.

One visible response was that Issei parents came down to the county courthouses in large numbers to register the births of children born in the United States but not previously recorded. One researcher noted that there were more births registered in 1914 in Santa Cruz County than there were babies actually born, a testimony to the Issei realizing the importance their America-born children would play in their futures.

Most historians have dismissed California's 1913 Alien Land Law as a hollow victory for the anti-Japanese forces, noting that the Japanese could easily avoid the law by either forming corporations with 51% American citizens as directors or putting the land in the name of their children. But the Alien Land Law was an emotional blow to the Issei in the region. Their access to opportunity was narrowing. Unable to immigrate freely from Japan, ineligible to become naturalized American citizens, and unable to either own land or lease it long-term, the future of the Issei grew darker by the year.

World War I volunteers leaving Santa Cruz, spring, 1917. The Japanese quickly registered for the draft as required by law, and a number of Issei attempted to volunteer for military service. Most of the Issei volunteers were rejected for military service.
SPECIAL COLLECTION, UCSC

JAPANESE AND WORLD WAR I

World War I had several important effects on the lives of the Japanese in the Monterey Bay Region. First, as we have already seen, the decline of the European salmon market hurt the Monterey salmon fishing industry, and many of the Japanese salmon fishermen had to shift to other pursuits. The war was a boon to Japanese farmers, however, as prices rose steeply following 1914. From that year until the end of the war, the Japanese moved to expand their investments. Because Japan was a member of the Allies, the war muted the anti-Japanese rhetoric in the region and also provided the local Japanese with an opportunity to demonstrate their loyalty to the United States.

WORLD WAR I AND THE ANTI-JAPANESE MOVEMENT

Japan was obligated by a mutual defense treaty with Great Britain to declare war on Germany in 1914. Japan was also motivated by the possibility of acquiring German possessions in East Asia at the war's conclusion. Thus when the United States officially declared war on Germany in April of 1917, Japan became an ally of the United States.

The United States government moved quickly to suppress any dissent regarding the war effort, and laws were passed making it illegal not only to protest the war but also to criticize any of America's allies. Since Japan was one of those allies, the espionage and sedition laws also silenced criticism of Japan. For the duration of the war, the attacks on the Japanese in the regional press stopped.

WAR EFFORT AND THE DRAFT

Japanese organizations in the United States immediately pledged their full support to the war effort in the spring of 1917. The Japanese Association of America declared that "when America faces an emergency, we cannot but rise as one to offer our humble services for the cause of our adopted 'Land of the Free and Home of the Brave'!" Local Japanese associations quickly followed suit, and during the various Liberty Loan drives in 1917 and 1918, the Japanese communities subscribed liberally and often.

The Japanese also responded quickly to the requirement that all males between the ages of twenty-one and thirty register for the draft on June 5, 1917. Almost all of the Japanese registrants were Issei and considered ineligible for military service. In one instance in Salinas, an Issei went before the draft board and requested to be allowed to naturalize so that he might be permitted to join the service, but the board denied his request.[39]

ISSUE OF LOYALTY

Many of the Issei members of the community saw World War I as an opportunity to prove, once and for all, that their loyalty was with the United States. As Kiichi Kanzaki, General Sec-

retary of the Japanese Association of America, put it in 1917, "I am happy to feel that America's entrance into this war gave a fair opportunity to test the true attitude of the Japanese toward America."[40] Regional communities contributed sums of money to support Liberty Loan drives and the Red Cross, which were well beyond their numbers. The little community of Japanese at San Juan Bautista contributed $2,700 to the first Liberty Loan Drive during the war, and all thirty-three men living there registered for the draft in June 1917.[41]

Few Nisei in the United States had reached military age by the time the United States entered the war in 1917. One young man, believed to be the first Nisei to enter the service during the war, was quoted in San Francisco as saying:

> It is an honor for me that I can go as the first American-born Japanese. I will do my very best and when duty calls me I will lay down my life for the cause of humanity and democracy. I pledge that I will bring no dishonor to the land of my birth or to the country of my forefathers.[42]

CITIZENSHIP THROUGH MILITARY SERVICE

In May of 1918 Congress amended the naturalization statutes to allow aliens who received honorable discharges from the United States military to apply for and receive their United States citizenship. Several Issei used this avenue to acquire their citizenship, including Jisaji Taoka of Watsonville and Ichiro Sakae of San Juan Bautista.

THE AMERICAN FLAG

From their first arrival in the region, the Japanese prominently displayed the American flag at every opportunity. With the United States at

ISSEI PARTY, WATSONVILLE, SUMMER, 1918

Clock
on the wall reads
11:45, and judging by the
light streaming in the
window, it is 11:45 A.M.
This is a lunch.

Telephone.
There were 26 telephone
numbers assigned to people with
Japanese surnames in Watsonville
in 1918. A telephone call to Santa
Cruz cost 15 cents, which is the
equivalent of $1.00 in
1996.

Flags. The
party is celebrating
Taoka's joining the
United States army. The
relative sizes of the two flags
is appropriate for the
moment.

Jisaji Taoka
was 29 years old and
is obviously the guest
of honor at this
event.

Photo of Temple. The
Buddhist temple in the photograph
was probably in Japan, as neither the
temple in Watsonville nor any of the
other temples in the United States
were this large.

Eye Contact.
Note that six of the eight
young men are consciously
looking away from the camera.
The Japanese reluctance to make
direct eye contact often carried
over into group
photographs.

Shot cuffs.
Issei men were very style
conscious. Note the very
proper cuffs and
cufflinks.

Gifts.
Gift-giving was (and is)
a basic element of Japanese
culture. The gifts were
probably given by the group to
Taoka in honor of the
occasion.

Beer bottles.
Japan had a long
brewing tradition, and these
Issei apparently had quite a
taste for America-brewed Acme
beer. Note the filled glasses
on the table.

Unknown fruit.
These may be persimmons,
which the Japanese often
used as decorative elements
on table settings.

Box lunches.
Called "bento," the
box lunch consisted of
an assortment of delicacies,
including the distinctive round
sushi which can be seen in this
box. Note ends of chopsticks
protruding beyond edge
of table.

PHOTO CREDIT: BILL TAO

war, July 4, 1917, took on extra significance, and the Japanese Association of Watsonville rose to the occasion by fashioning an American flag, which was forty feet wide and sixty feet long, for the parade on that day. Carried by twenty-four Japanese girls, the flag was deemed a "splendid parade feature" by the usually anti-Japanese Watsonville newspaper.[43]

AGRICULTURAL EXPANSION DURING WORLD WAR I

The war brought sudden prosperity to many of the Japanese farmers throughout the region. Prices of many agricultural products shot up, and small white beans, which the Japanese had

Ichiro Sakae, native of Hiroshima, came to the United States in 1905. At the age of 31 he volunteered for the United States Army and after being honorably discharged at the end of World War I, he applied for U.S. citizenship. Because his papers were not entirely in order, he had to reapply for citizenship in San Benito County in 1937. On December 7, 1937, Sakae was granted his U.S. citizenship.   SAKAE FAMILY

been growing and selling for 2.5 cents a pound in 1913, were selling for 15 cents a pound in 1916. Buoyed by the higher prices and a belief that the war would last for some time, the Japanese farmers began mortgaging both land and crops to expand their acreage.[44] In 1918 two Japanese farmers signed a ten-year lease on 264 acres of land near Castroville, agreeing to pay $25 per acre each year on land that previously had rented for $9 an acre.[46]

Issei Soldier, World War I. Jisaji Taoka, a Watsonville resident and native of Hiroshima, enlisted into the United States Army in July of 1918. Taoka was 29 and 1/2 years old when he enlisted, and this photograph was taken in September of that year. Taoka received an honorable discharge in March of 1919, and in June of that year he applied for and was granted U.S. citizenship.[45]   BILL TAO

In August of 1917 the Japanese Association of Watsonville placed an advertisement in the local newspaper asking anyone having land to lease to call the association.[47] The editor of the *Watsonville Pajaronian* observed optimistically that the agricultural market was "never better since the demand to feed both our armies and the European nations will continue for years to come."[48]

Japanese strawberry growers even leased land in and around Santa Cruz during World War I, including land just north of Mission Hill and acreage on the west side of town near the city limits.[49]

The prices did not hold for "years to come." In fact they barely held for one more year. With the end of the war in November of 1918, prices began to slide and the country plunged into an economic recession. Japanese farmers could not meet the payments on their outstanding loans, and during the early 1920s, scores of them lost property through foreclosure. Regional county deed books contain hundreds of such foreclosure for 1920, 1921, and 1922.

THE ANTI-JAPANESE MOVEMENT RESUMES - 1919

It did not take long after the war's sudden end on November 11, 1918, for the anti-Japanese movement to resume its campaign. As the United States slid into a year marked by lynchings, anti-Communist mobs, and a general fear of all things foreign, the anti-Japanese movement moved into high gear.

Behind the leadership of Senator James D. Phelan, the California-based Japanese Exclusion League put forth a broad anti-Japanese program that included the cancellation of the Gentleman's Agreement and a proposed amendment to the U.S. Constitution to prevent America-born children of Japanese immigrants from becoming United States citizens.[50]

THE MONTEREY COUNTY FARMERS POLL, 1919

Though public opinion polls were not commonly taken in 1919, a questionnaire distributed among farmers in Monterey County provides an excellent example of the popular feeling of the time. To the question "Should Japanese be excluded from land ownership in California?", 29 of the 32 respondents answered "yes." Another measure of the strength of feelings against the Japanese was the fact that 30 of the 32 farmers favored the resumption of Chinese immigration.[51]

THE ALIEN LAND LAW OF 1920

The Native Sons of the Golden West, the Native Daughters of the Golden West, the American Legion, and the California State Grange led a signature-gathering campaign in late 1919 to put an initiative before the California voters to further restrict the Japanese in California. Often called the Second Alien Land Law, the law contained four main provisions:

1. No land could be transferred to Japanese aliens.
2. No land could be leased by Japanese aliens.
3. No land could be owned or leased by corporations in which Japanese had the majority of stock.
4. Aliens could not act as guardians for citizens in matters concerning landownership.

The Japanese associations responded to the campaign by taking out ads in local newspapers urging voters to reject the proposition. The outcome of the vote was never in doubt, and the proposition received 75% of the vote throughout the region.

The intent of the Alien Land Law of 1920 was to drive the Japanese out of farming in California, and the law effectively ended the leasing of land by Issei. The Japanese associations responded by taking the issue into the courts, but they were unable to break the leasing restrictions in the law.[52]

The Japanese government responded to all the anti-Japanese activity in 1919 and 1920 by voluntarily terminating the emigration of photo brides in the spring of 1920. Japan was afraid of the harm that would come to their growing international stature if the United States finally passed an exclusion law similar to that passed against the Chinese in 1882. Thus, except for a few specialized categories, Japanese emigration to the United States was all but stopped after 1920. The Japanese government officials reasoned that if they voluntarily put an end to Japanese immigration to the United States, there would be no need for an exclusion act. They were wrong.

THE QUOTA ACT OF 1924 AND THE EXCLUSION OF THE JAPANESE

The early 1920s was a period of anti-foreign hysteria in the United States. Fueled by such organizations as the American Legion and the Ku Klux Klan, the American public struck out against all things foreign. The frenzy reached a climax when the United States Congress passed the Quota Act of 1924. Finally, the preference which the people of the United States had for immigrants from Northern and Western Europe was put into law. Southern and Eastern European countries had small quotas, while those such as Ireland and Great Britain had large quotas. Countries whose immigrants were "aliens ineligible to citizenship" were given no quotas. Thus, without being named specifically, the Japanese were excluded from immigrating to the United States. [See Appendix D. pp. 145-146, for further details on the 1924 law.]

The Quota Act was particularly galling to the Japanese government, for they had been voluntarily restricting and controlling emigration to the United States since 1900. All the delicacy and face-saving that had gone into the formulation of the Gentleman's Agreement was nullified, and Japan's response was an angry one. Huge rallies were held throughout Japan to protest the act, and July 1, 1924, was declared a National Humiliation Day because of the insult done to Japan by the United States government.

For some Japanese in California, the Quota Act was the final blow, and they pulled up stakes, gathered up their Nisei children, and returned to Japan. Others looked to other overseas Japanese communities, such as Brazil or Manchuria, for new opportunities.

The majority stayed, however, convinced that their future now lay almost completely in their America-born children, the Nisei.

SUMMARY

Because of a quirk in the Gentleman's Agreement that allowed Japanese women to come to the Monterey Bay Region, the period 1907 to 1925 was characterized by the growth and development of Japanese families. With their new added responsibilities, the Issei worked even harder to carve out niches in the regional economy. Unfortunately, their efforts only hardened the resolve of the anti-Japanese forces in California to limit and restrict the lives of the Japanese; by 1925, Japanese immigration had been stopped completely. And, the war clouds which had been developing in Asia were growing ever higher.

5 NISEI GENERATION
1925 TO 1940

Hemmed in by restrictive laws and ordinances, isolated by exclusion and an ever worsening international situation in Asia, the Issei felt increasingly trapped in America. The Japan that they left was changing rapidly, and like creatures frozen in amber, the Issei were suspended in time.

During the 1920s and 1930s, the Issei turned to their children as the only hope for a future in America. This period marks the beginning of the passing of the baton of leadership from the aging Issei to their America-born, American citizen children.

The Nisei attempted to jump into the American mainstream with both feet. They took on American nicknames, played basketball and baseball, joined the Boy Scouts (though in segregated all-Japanese troops), registered to vote, and pledged allegiance to the country of their birth. The Nisei organization, the Japanese American Citizens League (JACL), will represent the desire of the Nisei to become full-fledged American citizens. Or at least be allowed to make the attempt.

Spared the direct effects of alien land laws and immigration restrictions, the Nisei ran into their own obstacles of segregated schools, job discrimination, and segregated housing.

With one foot in their American classroom, the other in a Japanese-speaking family at home, the Nisei believed that hard work and patriotism would eventually open the doors to the American dream.

Two Nisei children, Salinas, c. 1930. Children like these carried the hopes and dreams of the Issei.   TAKANO FAMILY

THE JAPANESE POPULATION IN THE REGION

The 1920 manuscript census provides the last detailed snapshot of the Japanese communities in the region. Not surprisingly, the region's three primary agricultural valleys had the largest Japanese populations. The following numbers include the Japanese living both in the rural districts and the cities:

Pajaro Valley....................................1,032
Salinas Valley...................................785
San Juan Valley 286

Thus, of the 3,060 Japanese enumerated in 1920, over half were living in the region's agricultural areas, a reflection of the importance that farming held for the Japanese.

The other large concentration of Japanese was on the Monterey Peninsula, with 464 Japanese living either in Monterey, New Monterey, or the Carmel Valley. Fishing or cannery work was the predominant occupation listed for the Japanese living in that area, though there are a number of truck farmers listed just east of Monterey and in the Carmel Valley.

JAPANTOWNS

From their first arriving in the region in the 1890s, the Japanese resisted the high concentrations of population that had characterized the Chinese before them. Instead, the Japanese population gathered in loose clusters around the two primary areas of employment— farming and fishing—but their Japantowns did not have the con-

centration of populations as did their Chinese counterparts. The three main reasons for this:

1. The desire to be different and distant from the Chinese. All early Japantowns began in the segregated and low-rent districts that the Chinese had staked out in the nineteenth century. As their numbers grew in the twentieth century, the Japanese quickly dispersed. In Watsonville, for example, the Japanese moved north across the Pajaro River into Watsonville proper, despite the grumbling of the local newspaper.

2. Land tenure patterns. Many Japanese moved from laborers into either landownership or leaseholding, a pattern which often required their living on the land they worked. Where Chinese farm laborers continued to live in bunkhouses in the region's Chinatowns, the Japanese scattered out onto the fields, often living there all year.

3. Families. Perhaps the strongest force working to disperse the Japanese away from the Japantowns was each year's growth in the number of Japanese women and children. Issei parents felt much more comfortable raising their families beyond the immediate reach of Japantown's gambling halls and other sources of adult entertainment. Put

JAPANESE IN THE MONTEREY BAY REGION CENSUS STATISTICS, 1920-1940

	1920	1930	1940	%US Born 1940
Monterey Co	1,614	2,271	2,247	(1,530) 68%
San Benito Co	427	559	526	(381) 72%
Santa Cruz Co	1,019	1,407	1,301	(931) 72%
Total	3,060	4,237	4,074	(2,842) 70%

simply, Chinese lived, shopped, and socialized in Chinatown; the Japanese shopped and socialized in Japantown but lived elsewhere.

JAPANTOWN, WATSONVILLE

The largest urban concentration of Japanese in the region was in Watsonville, with over four hundred Japanese living in the city limits. Focused in an area of south Watsonville just east of Main Street, Watsonville's Japantown included a number of service businesses—barbers, tailors, merchants, doctors—along with the Buddhist temple, Presbyterian church, a Japanese Hall (where entertainment was provided), saloons, and pool halls. Prior to 1924 most of the gambling halls were Chinese owned and across the river in Brooklyn, but following the fire that destroyed much of the old Chinatown that year, the Chinese gamblers relocated along south Main Street. The Japanese wryly referred to the Chinese gambling joints as their "Hong Kong Bank."

By the 1930s most of the Chinese had moved back across the river, and the south section of Watsonville was a multicultural neighborhood. As Duncan Chin describes it in his book *Growing Up on Grove Street*:

> I grew up [in south Watsonville] with Chinese, Japanese, Filipinos, Mexicans, Slavs, Okies, blacks, and off-whites. It was a world of migrant farm workers and other folks struggling to survive the Great Depression.[1]

JAPANTOWN, MONTEREY

The second largest Japantown was in the area bounded by Franklin, Washington, and Tyler Streets in Monterey. This Japantown formed along the edges of the Chinatown created by the fire of May 1906, which destroyed the Chinese village in Pacific Grove. Again, this was primarily a service community with Japanese families living nearby. David Yamada indicates that there were about two-dozen retail businesses in Monterey's Japantown. He also suggests that there was a prefectural difference in the Japanese communities on the Peninsula, with Wakayama folks living primarily in the Monterey Japantown and Hiroshima migrants living in New Monterey.[2] Fishing was the primary occupational focus of the Japanese living in Monterey.

There was another, smaller cluster of Japanese living in New Monterey just above the canneries. The 1920 census lists several families on Ocean View (now Cannery Row) and Foam and Wave Streets, intermingled with Chinese, Azorean, Spanish,

Several all-Japanese baseball leagues were set up in the region, including teams such as this one from Watsonville.   BILL TAO

and Italian folks also employed in and about the canneries.

JAPANTOWN, SALINAS

Salinas' Japantown began when some of the early Japanese immigrants rented some run-down buildings across Lake Street from China-town. As its name suggests, Lake Street bordered on Carr Lake, a lagoon that filled with Salinas River overflow almost every winter. The 1920 census lists a remarkable cross-section of occupations, including doctor, shoemaker, tailor, carpenter, mechanic, barber, cook, and florist. According to preliminary analysis, Salinas' Japantown had the smallest concentration of workers employed elsewhere. Only 15 of the 177 Japanese listed themselves as laborers, an extremely low percentage. It appears that most of the Japanese families living in the Salinas area lived in semirural neighborhoods north and east of the city.

JAPANTOWN, SAN JUAN BAUTISTA

The cluster of Japanese businesses and families at the south end of Third Street in San Juan Bautista was the region's smallest definable Japantown. Anchored by Kichigoro Tanimura, the fifty-three-year-old, Hiroshima-born entrepreneur, the small community was the centerpiece for the Japanese living and working in the San Juan Valley. Tanimura had a small grocery with an *ofuro* (Japanese bath) in the back. The 1920 census lists a fish dealer, pool hall owners, several other merchants, and a cluster of farming families living at the south end of San Juan Bautista. Most of the San Juan Japanese were from Hiroshima prefecture.[3]

Salinas Japantown, c. 1911. The Japanese lived in the buildings on the left which backed up to the seasonal lake.   MONTEREY COUNTY HISTORICAL SOCIETY

RESTRICTIVE COVENANTS AND SEGREGATED HOUSING

The California society into which the first generation of Nisei emerged in the 1920s was a segregated one. Education, employment, and housing were all limited either covertly or by law. Whether foreign or United States born, all Asians were aware that they had a "place" in the California landscape, and the Monterey Bay Region was no exception.

Just as their Issei parents had not been willing to live in existing Chinatowns, the Nisei wanted the freedom to raise their families wherever they wished. Since the United States Supreme Court had made it clear in 1890 that ordinances that defined and "contained" Chinatowns were not constitutional, realtors and landowners in California maintained segregated communities by including restrictive covenants in leases and deeds.

Deed restrictions were quite common throughout the Monterey Bay Region, beginning with the flurry of developments in the region following World War I. In Santa Cruz County, for example, there were a number of coastal developments in the mid-1920s that routinely included deed restrictions.

Lots sold in Capitola in 1925 by the Bay Head Land Company contained the following sentence: "Property not to be sold, transferred, leased, rented or mortgaged to any other than Caucasian race, except servants." Similar statements can be found in deeds issued in Aptos and elsewhere in the region. The burgeoning

development in Rio Del Mar included not only restrictions on the type of house which could be built ("Spanish style architecture") but also the phrase, "no property transferred to other than Caucasians."[4]

Restrictive covenants were easy to boilerplate into the deeds of new developments, but it was more difficult to enforce segregation in older areas, particularly when the Japanese were willing to pay higher prices to rent or purchase the property. One such area was Santa Cruz County's Live Oak district, a mixture of farms and residences between Santa Cruz and Capitola. In a letter to the *Santa Cruz Sentinel* newspaper in 1922, in which he urged fellow citizens to "wake up," Santa Cruz real estate broker Eugene Cureton admitted that "the people of Live Oak district and surrounding country have an agreement to keep out the Japanese and to encourage white people to locate in [the] district." Raising the specter that the Japanese would build "shacks" and open their own stores, Cureton suggested that readers go out to see the "good American homes" on Seventh Avenue, with their "well kept lawns, flowers and good roads."[5]

Cureton's letter came as the result of a campaign mounted by the Live Oak Parent-Teacher Improvement Club earlier that month. In the midst of a meeting (which included a discussion about what kind of wax to use on the Live Oak school floor), Cureton brought the "Jap situation" before the organization. The group voted unanimously in favor of drafting a petition pertaining to the "elimination of the Jap in this section."[6]

Rio Del Mar, Aptos, c. 1926. Japanese were excluded from buying or renting property in developments like this because of restrictive covenants in the deeds.   DON HAILE COLLECTION

THE KU KLUX KLAN

The Ku Klux Klan is most often associated with the South, but during the 1920s it became a vigorous national organization with local chapters located throughout California. The 1920s Klan was a powerful nativist organization reflecting the growing anti-foreign sentiment that was sweeping across the United States. According to Article II of the Klan's by-laws, the organization was committed to "white supremacy" and "pure Americanism."[7] The Klan targeted Catholics, Jews, and foreigners in general as it recruited in California, and since there were few blacks or Jews living in Santa Cruz County in the 1920s, its primary adversaries were Catholics and Japanese. The Klan held several rallies in Live Oak in 1924, in which "highly anti-Catholic" presentations were made,[8] and Live Oak old-timers still remember that the Klan also targeted Japanese landowners in its meetings. Several cross burnings were held in the 1920s on a hill overlooking the district, and the Klan counted several hundred members in Live Oak during those years.

KKK parade, Stockton, 1925. This rare photograph shows the strength that the Klan had in many California cities. Similar Klan events were held throughout the Monterey Bay Region in the 1920s, and Japanese immigration was one of their targets.   NUTTER FAMILY

It is not clear exactly what effect the Klan had on the Japanese residents of the county, but the organization certainly reflected the general anti-immigrant, antiforeign feelings that were expressed in the 1924 Quota Act.

EDUCATION OF THE NISEI

Modern educational practices were a large part of the reforms that came to Japan following the Meiji Restoration in 1868, and the Issei immigrants understood the value of education, even if they were not fortunate enough to have gone to school themselves. The question which arose early in this century was a basic one: What should the Nisei be taught? Some Issei supported the position that the children should be educated with an eye to their eventually returning to Japan, while others advocated preparing their children for life in America. What eventually emerged was a compromise— the children should be educated in American public schools and then attend after-school Japan-

Japanese school, Watsonville, 1920s.   BILL TAO

ese schools to get a grounding in Japanese language and culture. [9]

Over the years, as the future of the Nisei in America became more important, support in the Japanese community shifted to favor the public school position, but Japanese schools played a major role in the education of the Nisei up to World War II.

The Nisei grew up in bilingual households. Most educational studies undertaken in the early twentieth century recognized that the Nisei (and their Chinese counterparts) were "handicapped in the lower grades by their poor knowledge of the English language." If the Nisei stayed in school, however, by the seventh year of school, they were able to overtake their non-Japanese contemporaries.[10]

Educators debated over whether the Japanese students should be "mainstreamed" or taught by themselves in separate rooms, and each school district handled the situation as they saw fit. One solution available to school districts with large Japanese populations was to establish completely separate Japanese schools.

All-Japanese segregated school on the west side of Watsonville, 1920s.   BILL TAO

SEGREGATED SCHOOLS

Segregated schools were nothing new in the Monterey Bay Region. When the Watsonville school district was faced with a sizable group of African Americans in the late 1860s, it established (with the support of the African American parents) a separate "Colored School." This school operated for approximately ten years until the black community had a change of heart and successfully forced the Watsonville school board to integrate their schools.[11]

The only place where the issue of separate schools for Chinese children came up was in Monterey, the only city with a sizable percentage of Chinese families. Many of the Chinese children received their education at a mission school established by religious groups in Pacific Grove.[12]

The United States Supreme Court, in *Plessy v. Ferguson* (1896), reaffirmed the constitutionality of segregated schools as long as they were "separate but equal." The state of California allowed local school districts to establish separate schools:

Segregated School, Watsonville, 1920s.   BILL TAO

"The governing body of the school district shall have power . . . to establish separate schools for Indian children and for children of Chinese, Japanese, or Mongolian parentage."[13] (It was the establishment of just such a school that precipitated the ruckus between the San Francisco School Board and Teddy Roosevelt in 1906.)

Preliminary research suggests that the only completely segregated Japanese public school was in Watsonville. Interviews with older Japanese residents and community photographs indicate that there was such a school out on the west side of the city in the early 1920s. It may have been that the elementary school in question just happened to reflect the heavy Japanese population in that area. Only after a review of the school district board minutes can we be certain. At least one elementary school in Salinas was also heavily Japanese, but again, we cannot be certain whether the school was actually segregated or not.

JAPANESE SCHOOLS IN THE REGION	
Hollister	(dates unknown)
Monterey	(early 1920s - 1942; 1963 - present)
Salinas	(1926 - ?)
Branch at Castroville	1936 - 1942
Branch at Chualar	dates unknown
San Juan Bautista	(pre-1920)
Watsonville	(1910 or 1919 to December 1941)

JAPANESE SCHOOLS

The first after-public-school Japanese school was established in Alviso in 1911, and soon there were numerous such schools throughout California. The curriculum focused on teaching the Nisei the Japanese language as well as traditional Japanese culture and geography. Eventually there were a number of Japanese schools throughout the region.

Those Japanese language schools which survived to December 1941 were quickly closed following the onset of the war with Japan. In some cases the Japanese language teachers in the schools were the first to be arrested by the FBI in the weeks following the attack on Pearl Harbor. The Japanese language schools had always been a target of anti-Japanese proponents throughout California, who

This building once housed the Japanese school in Castroville.   SANDY LYDON

argued that they taught not only culture but also obedience to the Emperor of Japan. There is no evidence to support this contention.

JAPANESE AMERICAN CITIZENS LEAGUE

As we have seen in the previous chapter, the Japanese associations were the most important community organizations in the first two decades of the twentieth century. The associations were lead by Issei, however, and focused on concerns of the Issei, including immigration and naturalization issues and relations with Japan. The Nisei had other concerns. Young professionals found their access to employment blocked at every turn, and even when they were able to achieve some economic success, there were neighborhoods in the region in which they were forbidden to live. Turned away at

Watsonville Nisei Boy Scout Troop, 1933. Organizations such as this helped young Japanese boys become part of the weave of American life.
TAMI YAGI COLLECTION

barber shops and swimming pools, the Nisei realized that they needed an organization to further their interests in the United States.

JACL FOUNDED, SAN FRANCISCO, 1930

There had been talk of forming a Nisei-centered organization as early as 1919, but it was not until 1928 that the New American Citizens League was formed in San Francisco. With a bow of respect toward their parents, the Nisei agreed that they would have to rely on the Issei for leadership, but "ultimately, the real solution would have to be made by the second generation members." Similar organizations popped up throughout the west, and at a convention in Seattle in 1930, most of them were joined together under the name, Japanese American Citizens League (JACL).

During its first decade, the JACL was non confrontational, with the leadership urging its members to focus on self-help and patriotism to open the doors that they found closed to them.[14]

WATSONVILLE CITIZENS LEAGUE, 1934

The momentum to form a Nisei organization in Watsonville came from the Issei, including Hatsusaburo Yagi, Ippatsu Jumura, Ennosuke Shikuma, and Ennosuke Fukuba. In 1934 these men invited Nisei leaders from the JACL to Watsonville, and after considerable discussion over an appropriate name, thirty-five Nisei formed the Watsonville Citizens League, with Tom Matsuda as its first president.[15]

The Watsonville Citizens League was primarily a social club during its early years. The Nisei took over building the floats for the July Fourth parades and held many picnics and socials. But still the leadership of the Japanese community remained in the hands of the Japanese association and the Issei.

SAN BENITO COUNTY JAPANESE AMERICAN CITIZENS LEAGUE, 1935

The first executive director of the national JACL was Saburo Kido, who assumed the position in 1934. Kido began writing letters to Nisei throughout the United States urging them to form chapters of the JACL, and his letters arrived in San Benito County in the spring of 1935. In June of that year, a meeting of young Nisei men and women was held in the Japanese School in San Juan Bautista, and after a brief discussion of Kido's letter, Joe Oshita made a motion to proceed with the formation of a JACL chapter.

Originally known as a Friendship Society, the chapter then assessed its members annual dues of $1 and joined the national JACL. As

Henry Omoto was one of the leaders of the San Benito County JACL during the late 1930s.   RUSSELL LEE, FARM SECURITY ADMINISTRATION

with other regional Nisei organizations, the San Benito County chapter focused on social events. Picnics and dances eventually evolved into public service projects, such as raising funds for Hazel Hawkins Hospital in Hollister. By the late 1930s, the monthly meetings featured speakers on self-help topics, such as "You and the Law" and "Nisei Marriage Problems," in which the topic of arranged versus free-choice marriages was discussed.

MONTEREY JAPANESE AMERICAN CITIZENS LEAGUE, 1932

Monterey's Nisei founded their chapter in January of 1932. Initially, the Monterey chapter's focus was much more directed to Issei concerns. The JACL members met to assist their parents in tax filings and other matters specific to the needs of the Issei.

Picnics and socials also dominated the Monterey JACL's agenda, but the organization also participated in local issues involving fishing rights and fair housing.[16]

AGRICULTURAL NICHE

During the 1920s and 1930s the Japanese continued to develop their niche in the region's agriculture. Strawberries and truck farming continued to occupy the bulk of their attention, though many still worked seasonally in the sugar beets and the region's orchards.

Agriculture in the Monterey Bay Region was constantly changing, and some of the Japanese farmers set aside small plots of acreage on which to experiment with new crops. Saburo Kitamura, for example, is credited with raising the first commercial broccoli crop in the Salinas Valley, in 1926. The impetus for the experimentation often came from Japanese agriculturists employed by the Japanese Association of America, in San Francisco. These men would travel throughout California, advising the Issei farmers about possible crops and how they might be grown in the region's excellent climate.

Japanese farmers are also credited with growing the first lettuce crop in the Salinas valley, in 1922, and the first green celery, in the 1930s. Crops such as these have become the mainstay of the Salinas Valley, which is now known as the "Salad Bowl of the World." By 1940 over half of all the strawberries, celery, snap beans, peppers, cauliflower, and spinach grown in California was grown by Japanese farmers.[17]

EFFECTS OF THE ALIEN LAND LAWS

Though the Japanese could avoid the alien land laws by recording their property in the names

JAPANESE FARM OWNERSHIP IN THE MONTEREY BAY REGION, 1940		
	Number of Farms Owned	Number Farmed As Tenants
Monterey County	21	104
San Benito County	3	34
Santa Cruz County	23	83
Region totals	47	221

of their children, not many of them took advantage of the loophole. The land laws and immigration exclusion retarded the evolution of the Japanese from farm laborers to tenants to landowners. In 1910, 11% of the Japanese farms were owned by the Japanese themselves. Had the progression toward ownership followed that of other immigrant groups, one would expect that by 1940 over half of the farmers would own their own farms. Yet, remarkably, in 1940 only 26% of the Japanese owned their own farms in California. The number was only 18% in the Monterey Bay Region, compared to an ownership of over 70% for all other farmers in the region.

Though Japanese farmed only a small percentage of the state's farms in 1940 and their farms tended to be smaller than most, they still wielded considerable economic clout because they were excellent farmers and produced a high volume of crop per acre. Non-Japanese farmers in the region found the Japanese to be formidable competitors, but they also admired their farming abilities. When asked about Japanese farmers, Pajaro Valley apple grower Luke Cikuth told an interviewer in 1964, "Japanese farmers from Japan, there's no question about it that they're the best . . . ."[18]

Agriculture continued to be the primary area of employment for both Issei and Nisei up to the beginning of World War II.

Japanese strawberry farmer, Soquel. The Japanese came to dominate regional strawberry growing up to World War II.   SPECIAL COLLECTIONS, UCSC

FISHING NICHE

During the 1920s and 1930s, the number of Japanese commercial fishermen in the region declined. Part of the reason for this decline was the ever increasing focus of the Monterey fish canneries on sardines and the large amount of money required to stay competitive in the business.

After 1929 the sardine industry was dominated by huge purse seiners, which required more capital than most Japanese could assemble.

Some of the Japanese fishermen remained to fish for rockfish, and a few pooled their resources and bought purse seiners. But most either left Monterey for the fishing grounds of Southern California (where they fished for albacore with hook and line, for example) or left fishing altogether.

Purse seiner at Monterey, c. 1930. The huge purse seiners became the standard in the sardine industry and not many Japanese followed the lead of the Italians to that level.

PHILLIPS COLLECTION, MONTEREY MARITIME MUSEUM

As alien land laws did not apply to fishing boats, the California legislature worked constantly throughout the 1920s and 1930s to fashion legislation either to tax heavily or eliminate the Japanese fishermen altogether. The proposed legislation usually revolved around the phrase "aliens ineligible for citizenship." The states of Washington and Oregon passed such laws, effectively driving the Issei out of their fisheries, but it was not until World War II (after the Japanese fishermen had been removed and taken to camp) that such a law was finally passed in California.

ABALONE NICHE: 1897 TO 1942

The Japanese dominated the hard-hat abalone industry from its inception at Point Lobos in 1897 to 1942. The Japanese abalone fishermen were tough, low profiled, and persistent, and, like the abalone they pursued, they locked on to their specialized niche and survived wave after wave of restrictive legislation. They knew that they could not defeat the forces of racism and restriction head-on, so they studied the industry, constantly adapting to changing conditions. Only the tsunami created at Pearl Harbor on December 7, 1941, was finally able to dislodge them. The history of the Japanese abalone diving industry in the Monterey Bay Region is a wonderful example of Issei values and sensibilities being reshaped and redefined by the California landscape.

A FEELING OF HOME

Point Lobos, fog, 1940. The landscape of the Monterey Peninsula looked strikingly similar to that of Japan.   NIELS IBSEN

Japan, fog. Painting by Hasegawa Tohaku bears a striking resemblance to Point Lobos on a foggy afternoon.   TOKYO NATIONAL MUSEUM

CALIFORNIA FISHING AND JAPANESE FISHING COMPARED

For most immigrants to California, whether from Europe or elsewhere in the United States, the state's coastal waters were an extension of the wide open American frontier. Anyone with the gear and access to the water could go whaling or fishing. Marine resources were limited only by one's imagination—everything was there for the taking in what seemed to be limitless quantities. The Euro-American (and to some degree the Chinese) fisherman was much like the American cowboy, the captain of his own ship, answering to no one and restrained only by the limits imposed by nature itself.

The Japanese immigrants saw the sea quite differently. The Japanese system of fishing

rights and access (called "sea tenure" by anthropologists), which was codified during the Tokugawa period, viewed the sea as an extension of the land. As such, the rights to the sea accrued to those living on the adjoining coast. Coastal villages controlled access, seasons, limits, and gear restrictions, and only fishermen in those villages were allowed to fish in the coastal waters. Only an estimated 10% of the Japanese population had access to fishing and whaling occupations.

In 1901 the Meiji government transferred the village rights to Fishing Co-operative Associations (FCAs), which continue to be responsible for coastal fisheries to this day.

Perhaps the most important attitude evolving from the Japanese system was the feeling of responsibility that Japanese fishermen had for the maintenance of the resource. Unlike the European, American, and Chinese fishermen who usually focused on taking as much from the sea as possible, it was not unusual for Japanese fishermen to argue in favor of conservation.[19]

This system was also designed to eliminate conflict on the sea and encourage cooperation. Perhaps more than any other fishermen in the world, the Japanese understood that they were all in it together.

For a Japanese fisherman, knowledge was essential, and nowhere was the Meiji spirit of scientific inquiry more apparent than in Japan's fishing industry. Universities and institutes were set up to study fishing. Many of the early Japanese fishermen who came to California were trained scientists, and once here, they continued their studies and adapted what they knew to this coast. As one non-Japanese fisherman in Southern California described it in the mid-1920s, "When a Japanese goes into [fishing], he goes in with the idea of learning all that is to be known. He knows the currents, tides, temperature of the water, winds, etc., and the effect of each upon the fish."[20]

The Japanese abalone divers who came to the Monterey Bay Region in the late 1890s were the most highly organized and efficient fishermen local residents had ever seen. Their amazement quickly turned to anger, however, as tons of dried abalone passed across the wharves destined to markets across the Pacific.

INEDIBLE ABALONE

The element which makes the following story so remarkable is that, in 1899, the vast majority of the residents on the Monterey Peninsula had no use for the abalone. Abalone is, after all, nothing but a large snail. Before the arrival of the Japanese, the only folks who had made any use of the lowly gastropod were the Indians and the Chinese. Local residents had watched with bemusement as the Chinese fishermen turned the abalone meat from something resembling (and as tasty) as the rubber in a boot into a hard lump that looked like a door knob. Though some observers grumbled about the possible decimation of the abalone as the Chinese assaulted them along the coast between 1854 and the 1880s, abalone fishing remained unregulated and

Japanese Divers and bunkhouse, Point Lobos, c. 1906. Note diving helmet on porch just left of dog and diving suits leaning against the wall, drying on the right.   PAT HATHAWAY

unrestricted until the arrival of the first Japanese divers in 1897.

Since locals didn't eat abalone, the movement to restrict the Japanese divers had very little to do with the abalone and very much to do with the Japanese.

RESTRICTION AND RESPONSE

Newspaper articles, which observed with curiosity and interest the Japanese abalone diving industry in 1897 and 1898, were using words of alarm by the summer of 1899. As wagon loads of dried abalone passed through Monterey bound for markets in San Francisco and beyond, the phrase "rapidly exterminating" entered the discussion of this new industry. [21]

A petition was circulated that asked the Monterey County Board of Supervisors to pass some kind of restrictive ordinance to protect this "delicious and valuable" resource.[22]

The remarkable debate that occurred before the Board of Supervisors between the Japanese divers and the local populace in the fall of 1899 brought the cultural differences into sharp relief. The Japanese came to the discussion armed with science and restraint. After highlighting the history of abalone diving in Japan and the life history of the various species of abalone found along the Monterey shoreline, the spokesman for the divers indicated that they were only taking the larger, older abalone. If left alone, the older abalone would died of old age and "be lost to the world." Managing the abalone and taking the larger stock actually increased the production of abalone. The Japanese concluded with a perfect statement of the Japanese attitude towards natural resources:

Point Lobos abalone divers, c. 1905. The success of these early divers brought immediate restrictions on their techniques.   KODANI FAMILY

[The abalone] is naturally given to us and we should make a profit out of it; if we leave them at the bottom of the sea we are [acting] against the will of God.[23]

The local newspapers dismissed the Japanese claims as a "fairy story" put forward by a "cunning" people.[24]

FIRST REGULATION

In October of 1899, in consultation with the Japanese divers, the Monterey Board of Supervisors passed the first abalone diving restrictions in the United States. The ordinance had two key elements: 1) Abalone diving was prohibited in Monterey County north of the Carmel River; and 2) abalone divers had to pay a license fee of $60 per year.[25] This meant that the Japanese could work the rocky uninhabited coast from Point Lobos south, and the good people of the Monterey Peninsula could have the abalone—which they didn't eat—around the Monterey Peninsula.

The state of California followed up in 1901 by passing restrictions limiting the size of abalone that could be taken by commercial divers to fifteen inches in circumference, or roughly eight inches in diameter.[26] Over the next forty years the abalone industry became the most rigidly regulated fishing industry in California.

When viewed against the white-hot flames of the anti-Japanese movement between 1900 and 1924, the evolution and survival of the abalone diving industry was remarkable. How, despite the flurry of regulations, were they able to do this?

First, the Japanese were already imbued with a conservation ethic. They were familiar with regulations, licenses, and controls and understood the importance of regulating the industry. This willingness to submit to regulation often disarmed their opponents and sent them back to their drawing boards to come up with something even more restrictive.

Second, the Japanese divers had American allies. The Japanese immigrants in the Monterey Bay Region could not have succeeded without American friends and allies to counter the attacks on their alienness. It took some courage in those days to befriend the Japanese. To do so meant running the risk of being called a "Jap-lover" and a traitor to the larger community. Just renting or leasing property to a Japanese was an act of enormous courage in white communities where the anti-Japanese fires burned hot. Yet, many did so, from lawyers willing to defend them to businessmen willing to

Japanese abalone diving headquarters and drying abalone, Point Lobos, c. 1910. California eventually passed legislation making abalone drying illegal.   PAT HATHAWAY

ABALONE RESTRICTIONS IN THE MONTEREY BAY REGION 1899 TO 1948

The following list reflects the major abalone legislation over the half-century that the Japanese divers worked in the region.
The regulations listed pertain only to the commercial diving for red abalone.

1899 - Commercial diving in Monterey County restricted to south of the Carmel River and in waters deeper than twenty feet.
       License fee of $60 per year imposed. (Monterey County)
1901 - Minimum size of 15 inches in circumference. (State)
1907 - Annual fishing license required. (State)
1909 - Minimum size of 17 inches in circumference. (State)
1911 - Illegal to bring abalone ashore dead or out of shell. (State)
1913 - Illegal to ship abalone out of California. (State)
1915 - Illegal to dry abalone in California, and illegal to ship abalone shells or meat out of the state. (State)
1917 - Minimum size of 7 inches in diameter. (State)
1921 - Illegal to take abalone between January 15 and March 15. (State)
1923 - Minimum size 8 inches in diameter. (State)
1939 - Commercial divers required to have special annual permit issued by the state. (State)

Abalone Shells, Point Lobos, 1930s. Piles of shells began to accumulate following the prohibition of shipping abalone products out of California in 1915.   KODANI FAMILY

form partnerships with them. The Japanese abalone divers had two very important friends and allies who helped and supported them through the difficult times.

The first, of course, was Alexander Macmillan Allan, the owner of Point Lobos and a partner with Gennosuke Kodani in the abalone diving business for over thirty years. Allan not only provided the Japanese abalone divers with a place, a refuge within which to develop their fledgling industry, but he made countless appeals throughout his life in favor of them and their industry. Allan touted the skills of the Japanese at every turn, gave tours and support to anyone who wanted to study the diving industry (many of the early studies of the abalone were done with his help), and lobbied for them in every venue imaginable. The depth of the Kodani-Allan alliance is reflected in a deep friendship between the two families that continues to this day.

The second friend was a German immigrant named "Pop" Ernest. Without "Pop" Ernest, it is unlikely that the abalone diving industry would have survived beyond the dark year of 1915.

DRYING AND CANNING TO 1915

Up to 1915, the bulk of each year's abalone catch was either canned or dried and shipped to China and Japan. But, as the list of laws shows, once the range of the divers was restricted and the minimum size of abalone was established, those advocating protection for the abalone focused on the destination of the finished product. Why did local residents so oppose the Japanese abalone diving industry?

1. A feeling of guilt about an unappreciated product. The fact that the abalone was so highly prized somewhere else made local residents nervous. "What did the Chinese and Japanese know that we don't?" they thought. The Euro-American residents of the Monterey Peninsula wanted the abalone precisely because someone else wanted them.

George Sterling, Carmel. Writers and poets such as Sterling helped make Monterey abalone famous throughout the world.   PAT HATHAWAY

2. The visible disappearance of intertidal abalone. As locals finally began to experiment with abalone, they denuded the local rocks of all abalone down to the low tide line. Despite both Japanese and American scientific evidence to the contrary, locals believed that abalone migrated from deep to shallow water, and the reason there were no abalone visible on the rocks was because the Japanese divers were depleting their deep-water sources. In a study done in 1917, a Stanford zoologist concluded that the intertidal abalone were disappearing because tourists and local residents were taking them. The Japanese divers were not the culprits, he said, and the abalone was in no danger of becoming extinct.[27]
3. The domination of the industry by the Japanese. The anti-Japanese movement targeted all of the economic niches which were developed by the Japanese.

CANNED AND FRESH ABALONE INDUSTRY, 1915 TO 1942

The abalone industry hit bottom around 1915, when the shipment of abalone products out of California was prohibited. There were not enough Chinese and Japanese living in California to consume all the abalone being harvested. The transition to another stage of the industry was provided by a man who eventually became known as the "Abalone King of Monterey."

"Pop" Ernest Doelter (see profile) was the second important non-Japanese ally who helped the Japanese abalone divers. Doelter was a huge, outgoing restaurateur who experimented with cooking abalone until he settled upon a straightforward and simple recipe. The abalone foot was cut into inch-thick slices, tenderized by pounding, breaded, and lightly fried. The

PROFILE: POP ERNEST, "THE ABALONE KING"

Pop Ernest was instrumental in turning the lowly abalone, described in 1900 as resembling part of a "rubber boot", into one of the most popular and sought-after delicacies in California. By popularizing the abalone, Pop Ernest extended the life of the Japanese abalone diving industry by over two decades. Over the years he developed an extremely close relationship with the Japanese divers and their families, and to this day the Japanese community recognizes the importance of his friendship and support.

Besides his size and personality, Pop Ernest's signature was a red fez which he wore in place of a chef's hat.   VERA STOKES

1870

Born in Germany. Birth name was Ernest Doelter.

1888

Immigrated to the United States, living and working as a caterer in New York.

1893

Became a naturalized United States citizen, after which he moved to California.

1906

Opened Cafe Ernest in downtown Monterey, where family tradition states that he discovered the need to tenderize abalone before cooking.

1913

Poet George Sterling composed "The Abalone Song" at Cafe Ernest.

1915

Introduced his abalone steaks in a San Francisco restaurant during the Panama Pacific International Exposition. Is convinced to stay in San Francisco to cook abalone.

1917

Returned to Monterey because of anti-German sentiment in San Francisco. Dropped the surname Doelter and becomes "Pop Ernest."

THE ABALONE SONG

Oh! some folks boast of quail on toast
Because they think it's tony;
But I'm content to owe my rent
And live on abalone.

Written at Ernest's Cafe,
Monterey, August 28, 1913
by poet George Sterling

1917 - 1918

Lived at Point Lobos where he continued to work on his abalone cooking recipes. Became good friends with Japanese abalone divers there. Sent fresh abalone steaks on ice to San Francisco restaurants where they became increasingly popular.

1919

Opened first restaurant on Monterey's Fishermen's Wharf known as "Pop Ernest's." His son, Ernest Doelter, Jr, did the cooking, while "Pop" did the promoting and marketing.

1920s

"Pop Ernest's" becames popular restaurant for the rich and famous. Writers, painters, and noted guests from the Del Monte Hotel came to enjoy his abalone and compose "abalone songs" in his guestbook.

1934

Died at Monterey.

1952

"Pop Ernest's" is sold and renamed Cerrito's.

recipe and process were really nothing new, as locals had done similar things to the abalone for years, but Doelter brought his gregariousness and powers of promotion to the industry.

Doelter's success at promoting abalone is proof that most things in business have to do with marketing and timing. His abalone promotion coincided with and was aided by the development of an artist-writer colony at Carmel after the turn of the century. His restaurant in downtown Monterey (he moved it to Fisherman's Wharf in 1919) became a popular hang-out, and by word of mouth and advertising, "Pop" Ernest elevated the abalone from "rubber boot" to epicurean delight.

This change in the status of the abalone had two major results. The first was breathing new life into a declining abalone diving industry. With export illegal after 1915, abalone canning steadily declined (the Point Lobos cannery closed in 1928), while the sale of fresh abalone grew steadily. The Great Depression put an end to the remaining abalone canneries in the region, but the fresh abalone business continued steadily until World War II. In the late

Slicing fresh abalone into steaks, Monterey, 1938. The steaks were then pounded and sold to restaurants.
PHILIPPS COLLECTION, MONTEREY MARITIME MUSEUM

1930s there were a dozen Japanese-owned abalone boats still working out of Monterey. The fact that the Japanese divers were woven into the fabric of the local tourism business helped insulate them from serious harassment.

The second effect was to increase the number of amateur abalone collectors along the coast. The State Department of Fish and Game spent the 1920s and 1930s trying to educate the public about the natural history of the abalone and keep both sport and commercial abalone hunters happy. But the abalone continued to be a conservation talisman up to World War II, with the public never completely understanding that it was the sportsmen and not the Japanese divers who were denuding the coastal rocks of the now-precious abalone. Even as late as 1938, the leading abalone expert in California said it quite simply: "The disappearance of the abalones [in the intertidal areas] can not be laid to the divers."[28]

ABALONE SHELLS

Abalone shells were an extremely valuable by-product for the Indians and Chinese prior to the arrival of the Japanese. The shells were a valuable trade item and over the centuries found their way along the coast and into the interior of the North American continent. The

Abalone shell pile, Seaside, 1931.
PHILIPPS COLLECTION, MONTEREY MARITIME MUSEUM

ABALONE BOAT, MONTEREY, 1931

Lampara Launch.
This small gas-powered lampara launch was used for catching sardines by the Sicilian fishermen.

The
Mother Boat.
These fifty-foot gasoline-powered boats carried the crew and catch while towing the small dive boat. There are five mother boats in this photograph. Can you find them?

Boom.
The long boom with its block and tackle was used to lift the live boxes out of the water for the trip back to Monterey.

Del Monte
Bathhouse.
The Del Monte Bathhouse was on the beach, while the hotel itself can be seen peeking through the trees on the right.

The Geneva.
This boat was one of about a dozen Japanese-owned abalone boats working out of Monterey in the 1930s. The boat was owned by Yaichi Takabayashi.

Dive Boat.
The Japanese divers worked off the smaller dive boat. The air was pumped to the diver by a small gasoline-powered compressor. The diver was usually attended by at least two men on the boat to maneuver it and insure the continued flow of air.

Live Boxes.
These boxes were placed in the water to hold and keep alive the abalone after they were taken. These live boxes were a 1930 innovation which extended the range of a typical diving expedition from two days to five or more days.

The Number.
Abalone fishing regulations required that the fishing license number be displayed in large numbers on the bow of the boat.

Copper Plate.
This plate helped protect the wooden boat from the constant pounding and scraping of the bags filled with abalone being dragged out of the water and into the boat.

PHILIPPS COLLECTION, MONTEREY MARITIME MUSEUM

Chinese sold the shells to button manufacturers and others who used the mother-of-pearl in making jewelry and furniture. The shells were also an important part of the souvenir business at Monterey and Carmel.

The Japanese also used the shells for jewelry manufacture, and tons of shells were shipped all over the world until the 1915 export prohibition began to take effect. The result was that by the 1930s the Monterey Peninsula was dotted with huge abalone shell mountains.[29] The prohibition of shipping abalone shell out of California was finally relaxed in 1941, but it is still not unusual to see abalone shell as decorations in walls and buildings in the region, most dating from before World War II.

IMPORTATION OF JAPANESE DIVERS

One of the greatest challenges for Kodani and others in the abalone business was keeping a steady supply of fresh, young Japanese divers. Nisei were not interested in the profession, and a decade's worth of diving was about all that a diver's body could endure. When the Gentle-

Roy Hattori, c. 1938. Hattori is believed to have been the only Nisei to become a professional abalone diver.

HATTORI FAMILY

man's Agreement went into effect in 1908, Japanese abalone divers could no longer enter the United States, and for a decade no new divers came into the business. But, with the burgeoning fresh abalone business in hand, the company owners appealed to the United States government to allow them to bring in replacement divers from Japan. The arrangement required both the Japanese government's assent (they issued the necessary passport) and the United States government's permission to land. Following World War I, all parties agreed to permit a limited number of divers to come to the United States to work for the Monterey abalone diving companies.

The United States government did not want these divers to circumvent the immigration prohibition, so they were allowed to come only with the understanding that they would eventually return to Japan. The Point Lobos Canning Company posted bond with the Immigration and Naturalization Service guaranteeing that the divers would return to Japan by a certain date; and during the 1920s and 1930s, several dozen Japanese divers came into the region as guest workers, returning when their allotted time expired. Again,

Japanese "mother" boat towing smaller dive boat off California coast, 1938.

PHILIPPS COLLECTION, MONTEREY MARITIME MUSEUM

such an arrangement could not have been negotiated had the Japanese abalone industry not been so interconnected with the Monterey Bay Region's economy. It is clear that if the abalone business had still been primarily for export, people like A. M. Allan would not have been able to make this special arrangement.

The Japanese divers were guest workers in every sense of the word, sending considerable amounts of money back to Japan while working on the Monterey Peninsula. For depression-battered families living in Chiba and Wakayama prefectures, the money from California was "priceless."[30]

Japanese historian Toshio Oba notes that an unknown number of divers also came into the United States illegally during the period, either as stowaways directly from Japan or through Canada or Mexico.[31]

The relationship between the divers and their hosts was often extremely close, and as will be seen in the next chapter, one of the divers from Chiba went to camp with the Kodani family rather than return to Japan during World War II.

INTERNATIONAL WAR CLOUDS

By the mid-1930s, the Japanese were woven into the economic and social fabric of the region. The anti-Japanese mutterings continued, but a begrudging respect had grown for these hard-working people whose kids seemed just like everybody else's. The Issei were still in charge within the Japanese community, but the Nisei were making steady progress, particularly under the leadership of the JACL. The Nisei seemed to be moving towards the mainstream of American society.

Unfortunately, the Japanese government was not making it easy for Americans to disconnect the Nisei from the home of their parents. Steadily, inexorably, the Japanese military moved onto the Chinese mainland. Following the bombing of Chinese coastal cities in 1937, Chinese Americans took to the streets throughout the United States to protest Japan's actions. Henry Luce, publisher of *Life* magazine, began a strong pro-China, anti-Japan

Japanese abalone dive boat working off the rocks south of Big Sur, 1938.

theme in his publications, and Pearl Buck forever immortalized the beleaguered Chinese peasant under the Japanese onslaught in her novel *The Good Earth,* which was made into a successful and popular movie in 1937. The result was that the image of the Chinese rose and that of the Japanese declined.

The winds of an Asian war began to fan the anti-Japanese embers into flame.

SUMMARY

The period 1925 to 1940 was one of consolidation for the Japanese in the Monterey Bay Region. The Issei continued to experiment and expand their niche in the region's agriculture, while adjusting to a lesser role in fishing. Most successful niches involved partnerships and collaborations with Americans. From agricultural cooperatives to abalone diving partnerships, many of the successful Japanese enterprises had American partners.

But the future rested squarely on the shoulders of the Nisei. Graduating from local high schools and moving on in increasing numbers each year to higher education, the Nisei carried the hopes and dreams of their parents.

The war clouds over Asia were troublesome, but many Issei took comfort in their America-born children. The Nisei were American citizens. The United States would certainly protect them if worse came to worst. Wouldn't it?

6 WAR YEARS
1940 TO 1945

In the spring of 1942, all the elements of the story of the Japanese in the Monterey Bay Region converged on the rodeo grounds at the north edge of Salinas. In a scene reminiscent of the conclusion of the *Tale of the Forty-Seven Ronin*, where the samurai march stoically through the streets of Edo, the Japanese community filed off the buses and into the barracks and horse stalls to begin what would eventually be over three years of restriction and confinement.

The removal of the Japanese from the West Coast was (and still is) unprecedented. Never before or since has an entire group been singled out and forcibly removed simply because of their physical appearance.

It is impossible to overstate the importance of World War II for the Japanese community. Everyone of Japanese ancestry left the region, leaving behind lives and businesses dating back almost half a century.

The wartime removal to concentration camps in the interior was an economic tragedy beyond measure for the Japanese community. But the emotional and psychological pain far outweighed the money. The community that valued loyalty above all else was accused of disloyalty. Heads held high, the Japanese did as they were instructed. It was their duty to do so.

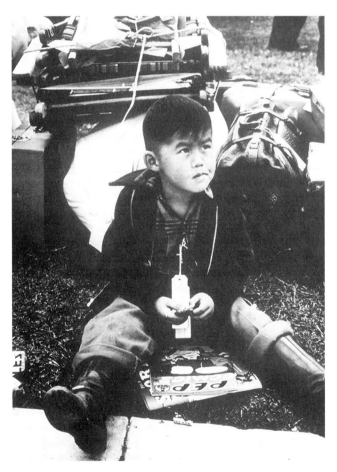

Unidentified young man waiting to be transported from downtown Salinas out to the temporary detention center at the rodeo grounds. May 1942.
FARM SECURITY ADMINISTRATION

PRELUDE 1940 - 1941

The American focus on Pearl Harbor usually obscures the fact that World War II began much earlier than December 7, 1941. Japan's 1937 attack on mainland China signaled the beginning of the war in Asia, while Nazi Germany's invasion of Poland in September 1939 marked the beginning of the war in Europe. Americans watched with fascination and horror as war engulfed most of the world.

PEACETIME DRAFT, SEPTEMBER 1940

The seriousness of the international situation was best demonstrated by Congress imposing

Young Nisei tagged prior to her removal to a concentration camp. She and her fellow prisoners had nothing to do with Pearl Harbor.
FARM SECURITY ADMINISTRATION

the first peacetime draft on September 16, 1940. Over 16,000,000 men registered for the draft. The National Guard was federalized, and throughout the Monterey Bay Region, young men began joining the armed forces to take care of what was then a one-year military obligation. The draft was to expire in September 1941, but world events convinced Congress to extend it, though the measure passed by only one vote.

A number of local Nisei were included among those who entered military service in 1940 and 1941, and young men in uniform became a common sight in every community in the region.

JACL AND THE JAPANESE AMERICAN CREED

The Nisei watched the international wars with growing concern. They knew that a war with Japan was a distinct possibility, and they continued efforts to reaffirm their loyalty to the United States. No document captures the feeling of the Nisei poised on the edge of war better than the Japanese American Creed, written by Mike Masaoka in the spring of 1941.

DECEMBER 7, 1941

There are moments in American history when time stops. Observers and participants seem frozen in mid-stride, and for the remainder of their lives, the participants can tell you exactly where they were, what they were doing, and what they were wearing. Pearl Harbor was such a moment.

Word of Pearl Harbor spread quickly throughout the region, and since it was a Sunday, many families spent the day together, talk-

---

JAPANESE AMERICAN CREED

I am proud that I am an American Citizen of Japanese ancestry, for my very background makes me appreciate more fully the wonderful advantages of this Nation. I believe in her institutions, ideal and traditions; I glory in her heritage; I boast of her history; I trust in her future. She has granted me liberties and opportunities such as no individual enjoys in this world today. She has given me an education befitting kings. She has entrusted me with the responsibilities of the franchise. She has permitted me to build a home, to earn a livelihood, to worship, think, speak, and act as I please—as a free man equal to every other man.

Although some individuals may discriminate against me I shall never become bitter or lose faith, for I know such persons are not representative of the majority of the American people. True, I shall do all in my power to discourage such practices, but I shall do it in the American way: above board, in the open, through courts of law, by education, by proving myself to be worthy of equal treatment and consideration. I am firm in my belief that American sportsmanship and attitude of fair play will judge citizenship and patriotism on the basis of action and achievement, and not on the basis of physical characteristics.

Because I believe in America, and I trust she believes in me, and because I have received innumerable benefits from her I pledge myself to do honor to her at all times and in all places, to support her Constitution, to obey her laws, to respect her Flag, to defend her against all enemies, foreign or domestic, to actively assume my duties and obligations as a citizen, cheerfully and without any reservations whatsoever in the hope that I may become a better American in a great America.

Mike Masaoka, Spring 1941

---

ing and wondering what would happen next. It was not a surprise that the United States was at war. This had been brewing for a long time. But now everyone's future was in doubt, and the conversations focused on self and family. Duncan Chin remembered clusters of adults,

Life magazine helped stir up the hysteria about the possibility of a Japanese attack on the United States mainland with drawings such as this. LIFE MAGAZINE

sitting and talking quietly throughout his South Watsonville neighborhood that afternoon. Like boxers trying to clear their heads after taking a solid punch, people shook their heads and worried about their future.

Ichiro Yamaguchi, thirty-three-year-old, Watsonville-born Nisei, learned about Pearl Harbor while attending services at the Presbyterian church:

> When Pearl Harbor was bombed I felt like somebody shot me. It was a bad feeling. I worried that something might happen to us....It was a Sunday and I was at church. In those days we had worship services together and it was crowded. They had the English service first and then the Nisei were excused....We stood outside talking and there were a lot of guys in uniforms already on account of the war with Germany. They were visiting here. The radio said, "All servicemen report back to your headquarters.[1]

Special editions of local newspapers were printed quickly so that by that evening, most everyone knew what had happened.

GROUND RULES FOR READING ON

Because this book is focused on the regional Japanese community, we will not have time to develop the entire story of World War II at home. There are some persistent notions and myths about World War II and the imprisonment of the Japanese which need to be dispelled at the outset. Those wishing to read further in the subject may consult the notes at the back of this book.

War with Japan was not a surprise. As noted earlier, relations between Japan and the United States had been rocky from the beginning of the twentieth century. It was a foregone conclusion that Japan and the United States would eventually clash over their competing interests in the Pacific Ocean. Thus, the United States government had been studying the Japanese community for years, discussing what might happen when the war with Japan eventually occurred. This helps explain why the government was able to move so quickly—arresting Japanese community leaders, for example,

before the day of December 7th was over. It also explains why the JACL and Japanese associations became increasingly nervous about events in China. The attack on Pearl Harbor was a surprise, but the war was not.

Fear of a Japanese attack in the Monterey Bay Region was very real. After years of interviewing hundreds of people living in the region during the war (including members of all regional communities), the one constant in the period immediately following December 7 is fear—fear caused by blackouts, air raid drills, submarine sightings, and news censorship. Coastal gun emplacements were set up immediately following Pearl Harbor, and volunteers patrolled area beaches and staffed observation stations atop local mountains. The fear and lack of information muted the fair voices which might have been raised as the Japanese were rounded up and moved off the coast. From this relatively safe location fifty years later, it is easy to wonder where the fair-minded guardians of civil liberties were hiding during the first half of 1942. The answer is very simple—they were worried about their own personal safety and futures. Would the Japanese attack California? Will I be drafted and sent to the Pacific?

This does not absolve their silence, nor excuse the extremely racist and ill-informed words and deeds committed during the war. But it does begin to explain HOW it happened.

The removal of the Japanese was illegal and there were United States government officials who knew it. Residents of

The attack on Pearl Harbor sent shock waves which were eventually felt in the Monterey Bay Region.

the Monterey Bay Region can be forgiven for not knowing any better, but the government, that last bastion and defense of civil liberties and freedoms, cannot be so forgiven. Recent research has brought to light the fact that the government deliberately lied to the Supreme Court when justifying the removal of the Japanese.[2]

No person of Japanese ancestry was ever charged. No person of Japanese ancestry was ever charged or tried for an act of espionage in the United States, Alaska, or Hawaii. None. Period. Myth and rumor still swirl around this period about local Japanese spies, submarines being refueled by Japanese fishing boats, and crops being grown in the shape of arrows to direct attacking Japanese aircraft to strategic sites. Despite the persistent mythology, no Japanese, citizen or alien, was ever charged or convicted of any acts of treason.

The Japanese living in the Monterey Bay Region had nothing to do with the attack on Pearl Harbor. The only connection between the Nisei spinach farmer and the pilot flying

The call to avenge Pearl Harbor will eventually spread to the innocent Japanese Americans in the region.

over Hickam Field was some shared physical characteristics. Nothing more. The events at Pearl Harbor resulted in the Japanese being removed, but there is no other connection. Thus, the comment usually made to justify the removal of the Japanese —"Compared to what happened to those unlucky souls at Pearl Harbor, the relocation of the Japanese was benign"—has no place in the discussion. The attack on Pearl Harbor was carried out by the government of Japan. The Japanese living in the Monterey Bay Region had nothing to do with it.

The Japanese were removed for their own protection. This rationalization was invented after the war. There was no discussion about the removal being for their own protection at the time. Most incidents of violence against Japanese occurred in the weeks immediately following the attack on Pearl Harbor. By the time that relocation began in April of 1942, the violence had all but stopped.

Besides, if the incarceration had been to protect the Japanese, then the stockades and enclosures would have been armed with the guns facing out. The guns were facing in.

Relocation was about race. No amount of twisting and turning can negate the fact that the removal of the Japanese during the war was racially motivated. As we shall see, all enemy

Front page of special edition of Watsonville newspaper published the evening of Sunday, December 7.   WATSONVILLE PAJARONIAN

aliens—German, Japanese, and Italian—were restricted in their movements and placed under curfew in early 1942. Over time, however, the Italians and Germans were relieved of the restrictions. Despite the fact that German and Italian spies were arrested in the United States and convicted of espionage, neither group was incarcerated. The Japanese were. It was, at bottom, a matter of race.

CALLS FOR RESTRAINT

During the first week following Pearl Harbor a number of community leaders, both Japanese and non-Japanese, called for local citizens to remain calm. On December 9, 1941, I. Motoki, the secretary of the Watsonville Japanese Association, issued a statement declaring his faith in the future: "I urge all Japanese persons in the Pajaro Valley to continue with their work and industry the same as heretofore since I am satisfied that we shall be fairly treated by the government, even though we may not be citizens of such nation."

In San Benito County, Henry Omoto, President of the local JACL, declared, "We have always been for the United States and what it stands for, and we are for it today, come what may."[3] On December 10, 1941, the editor of the Hollister newspaper reprinted an editorial from the *San Jose Mercury* which urged its readers not to succumb to hysteria and hate. "It does not make you a better American to toss an epithet at any person who looks like a Japanese. The presumption if you see them, is that they are as good Americans as you are—and are better Americans if you stoop from American tolerance to call them names."[4]

Meanwhile, all along the West Coast, the United States government was moving quickly.

THE FIRST WEEK: DECEMBER 7-14, 1941

The federal government acted very quickly, a testimony to the amount of research and surveillance focussed on the Japanese community prior to December 7. Using the 1940 census, alien registration records, and draft registration information, the government knew where every person of Japanese ancestry lived. The following timeline shows how quickly the government tightened restrictions on the Japanese community.

Photograph of bell tower at the Salinas Buddhist Temple after the gong was removed, published in *Life* magazine, March 9, 1942.   LIFE MAGAZINE

SUNDAY EVENING, DECEMBER 7

The FBI arrested 1,500 Issei throughout the United States. Most were leaders of the Japanese associations and Buddhist priests.

MONDAY, DECEMBER 8

United States land borders were closed to all enemy aliens and all persons of Japanese ancestry, both aliens and citizens. Issei bank accounts were frozen. Salinas Buddhist Temple is told to take down their large bronze gong, because Monterey residents were afraid it would be used to signal an invading Japanese navy.[5]

TUESDAY, DECEMBER 9

Nisei bank accounts were frozen. The freezing of bank accounts caused an incredible hardship

Shell crater left by Japanese submarine, Goleta, California, February 23, 1942.   LIFE MAGAZINE

on the Japanese community. Ironically, many local charities were severely hindered by the freezing of the bank accounts. The Japanese had been heavy contributors to various charitable fund raising drives, and the checks that they had given to organizations, such as the anti-tuberculosis fund, were not honored by the banks.

THURSDAY, DECEMBER 11

Defensive sea areas were set up and all boat traffic off the coast was restricted. All fishermen were required to obtain government permission to fish off the coast.

JAPANESE SUBMARINE IN MONTEREY BAY: DECEMBER 20, 1941

Rumors of a full-scale attack on California by the Japanese flew around the Monterey Bay Region during the early days of the war. The worst fears of local residents seemed to be realized on Saturday afternoon, December 20, 1941, when Japanese submarine I-23 surfaced alongside the oil tanker *Agiworld* off Cypress Point south of Monterey and began firing its deck gun at the unarmed tanker. After attempting to ram the submarine, the tanker zigzagged around the Monterey Peninsula and across Monterey Bay with the submarine in hot pursuit. Several dozen rounds were fired from the submarine's deck guns, landing all around the tanker but not hitting it.

Aptos resident Paul Johnston remembered the mood of the time and the sight of the tanker:

We were on needles and pins. We didn't know what would happen. And then I was out on the mail route up here on the [Aptos] Terrace, and I see this ship come flying across the bay wide open and the Jap submarine come up there right outside of Monterey. I think the submarine shot at that boat 26 times, but [the Japanese] were so nervous, too, that they didn't hit the boat.[6]

Japanese submarines were more successful elsewhere on the Pacific Coast, sinking several freighters during the early weeks of the war. Perhaps the most dramatic submarine attack came on February 23, 1942, when submarine I-17 surfaced off the oil fields just north of Santa Barbara and fired about ten rounds from its deck gun into the oil field before diving. This attack heightened the sense of fear and "needles and pins" which Paul Johnston remembered.

TIGHTENING OF RESTRICTIONS: TO FEBRUARY 14, 1942

Blackouts, air raid drills, and the training of local militia forces occupied the attention of local residents during the first weeks of the war. Though the federal government had not deter-

Nisei JACL members preparing a last picnic lunch for its members before being evacuated, May 1942. Appropriately, the lunch consisted of hot dogs. San Juan.   RUSSELL LEE, FARM SECURITY ADMINISTRATION

mined exactly what it would do about the enemy aliens living in the region, each day further restrictions were imposed on their movement and livelihoods. Enemy aliens included unnaturalized immigrants from Germany, Italy, and Japan.

- January 1, 1942 - All liquor licenses held by Japanese are canceled.

- January 5, 1942 - Enemy aliens must surrender firearms, weapons, or implements of war; ammunition; explosives or materials used in the manufacture of explosives; short-wave radio receiving sets; transmitting sets; signal devices, codes, or ciphers; cameras and papers, documents or books in which there may be "invisible writing...."

- January 15, 1942 - Enemy aliens required to get permission to travel more than five miles from their homes.

New Year's Eve, 1941. The Watsonville Young Buddhist Association dance band played as usual, but the celebration was much more restrained than usual.   BILL TAO

- February 2, 1942 - All enemy aliens over fourteen years of age required to re-register at the nearest post office.

- February 10, 1942 - FBI raided residences and businesses removing at least twenty men. Raids continued for several days.

- February 12, 1942 - Enemy aliens required to turn in all bows and arrows and flashlights.

- February 14, 1942 - Signs placed on local beaches ordering enemy aliens to stay away from the coast. Signs were printed in Japanese, German, Italian, and English.

Many Italian-owned purse seiners such as this one at Monterey were taken over by the government and used as coastal patrol boats during the war.   PHILIPPS COLLECTION, MONTEREY MARITIME MUSEUM

EXECUTIVE ORDER 9066

Much has been written about the decision to remove all Japanese, citizens and aliens, from the immediate West Coast of the United States.

Professor Roger Daniels, the preeminent historian on the subject of the decision, concluded that it was the United States military that argued longest and hardest for removal, while a small group of agencies and officials suggested that it would not be necessary. President Roosevelt eventually took the word of the military and on February 19, 1942, issued the executive order which set up the machinery under which the military would eventually act. The operative phrase in this decision was "military necessity."

RESPONSES OF THE JAPANESE COMMUNITY

Amid the FBI raids and increasing animosity of the local populace, the Japanese community leaders continued to make public statements about the loyalty of their organizations and their individual members. The first couple of weeks of the war were a fearful time for the Japanese. As their community leaders

Sicilian fishermen, Monterey, 1938. Many of these fishermen were moved away from the coast and their livelihoods.   PHILIPPS COLLECTION, MONTEREY MARITIME MUSEUM

were arrested one by one and taken away, they sought to find ways to convince their neighbors that they had nothing to do with anything going on in the Pacific.

WHAT COULD THEY HAVE DONE?

It is useful to take a minute and examine the options which were available to the Japanese community by early February 1942. The Issei could not leave the country or the region. With their bank accounts frozen, few families had the wherewithal to move had they been able to. The best they could do was stay low, tend to business, and hope that a sense of fairness would find its way into the discussion.

Statements of loyalty were met with suspicion and outright derision in some cases. Miller Freeman, the editor of *The Pacific Fisherman* the most influential fishing publication in America, wrote, "It is not enough for Japanese Americans to buy bonds and prate of loyalty. Words spoken and oaths sworn by Japanese tongues will bear little weight with the American people so long as Pearl Harbor reverberates in American memories."[7]

DAMNED IF THEY DID; DAMNED IF THEY DIDN'T

Surveys and analyses by the FBI and the California Attorney General's office confirmed what the Japanese themselves were saying—there was no evidence of espionage or sabotage by any members of the Japanese community on the Pacific Coast. Confronted with this information, several government leaders came to the conclusion that such evidence was proof that the group was, in fact, disloyal. In a statement before a congressional committee in February of 1942, California Attorney General Earl Warren put forward what later historians called "the paranoid rationale":

I believe that we are just being lulled into a false sense of security and that the only reason we

Some Japanese Americans, such as this one in Berkeley, attempted to remind the public that they were American citizens, but to no avail.
FARM SECURITY ADMINISTRATION

haven't had a disaster in California is because it has been timed for a different date....Our day of reckoning is bound to come in that regard.[8]

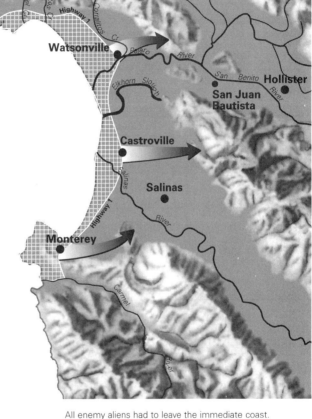

All enemy aliens had to leave the immediate coast.

ENEMY ALIENS MOVED OFF THE COAST: FEBRUARY 24, 1942

The government had been making threats to move all enemy aliens off the coast since mid-December 1941. In January of 1942 the government announced its intentions to proceed with such a removal, and by the end of the month had outlined its plans with the local newspapers.

Tommy Kadotani, spokesman for the small Japanese community in Santa Cruz, was quoted as saying, "I hope [the removal] doesn't come, but if it does we'll abide by the rules and take it." Robbie Ghio of the Santa Cruz Italian community that would also be affected by the ruling said that the Italians would "take it on the chin like a man."

RESTRICTED ZONE: FEBRUARY 24, 1942

In January of 1942 the government announced tentative plans to clear all enemy aliens from Santa Cruz and Monterey Counties. A vigorous protest from all affected parties caused the military to scale back the plan and remove the enemy aliens from just the immediate coast. The amended boundaries were published in

February with a deadline for removal of February 24:

Santa Cruz and Monterey Counties, including part of Santa Cruz and Monterey; commencing at the mouth of Laguna creek running up the creek to state highway No. 1 (coast road), then south on state highway No. 1 to the Carmel River and along the Carmel river to the Pacific ocean, then up the shoreline to the point of beginning.[9]

The order also contained a 9:00 P.M. curfew for enemy aliens living outside the restricted area: "An enemy alien found during the curfew hours anywhere except at his home or place of employment [will] be subject to immediate arrest and internment."[10]

Using alien registration cards and census data, the government determined that 1,462 Italians, 571 Japanese, and 83 Germans would have to move on or before February 24.[11]

"MALE NOTTE"—THE SAD NIGHT

The Italian fishermen in Santa Cruz and Monterey were severely limited by the restriction, as none of the Italy-born fishermen could use their boats or even be on the coast. Italian artichoke farmers and brussels sprout growers on the north coast of Santa Cruz county were also hard hit by the order. Most of the Italians lived on the west side of Santa Cruz inside Mission Street, so many of them were forced to move across Mission Street. Work schedules were disrupted, and even a simple trip to the post office was restricted by the order.[12]

The Japanese found themselves in similar circumstances. Nisei did not have to move beyond the line, but Issei did, so there were many instances where entire families moved, rather than be divided by Highway 1. Housing was difficult to find for both the Italian and Japanese aliens, and there were some instances of real estate agents taking advantage and rent gouging.

"VOLUNTARY" EVACUATION: MARCH 1942

In early March 1942, General John DeWitt, the head of the Western Defense Command, laid out the coastal zone from which he intended to remove all people of Japanese ancestry. But, citing that it was still "impracticable" for the government to undertake such a massive operation, General DeWitt suggested that those Japanese and other enemy aliens who might wish to move to the interior of the United States could do so. "Those Japanese and other aliens who move into the interior, out of this area now will gain considerable advantage and in all probability will not again be disturbed."[13]

As the news of this opportunity spread throughout the Japanese communities on the west coast,

Members of the San Juan Bautista Japanese community clean up the Japanese section of the cemetery prior to being interned, May 1942.   RUSSELL LEE, FARM SECURITY ADMINISTRATION

most community members realized that they could not take advantage of it. Not only were funds difficult to assemble for such a move, but the intermountain states of Nevada, Utah, and Idaho all made it clear that they did not wish the Japanese to settle there. One group which was able to make the move was put together by Fred L. Wada of Oakland. Wada eventually assembled 130 persons of Japanese ancestry from northern and central California and was able to negotiate a move to a farm in the small town of Keetley, Utah.

WATSONVILLE JAPANESE ALMOST MOVE TO IDAHO: MARCH 1942

In early March of 1942, with most of their Issei leaders removed by the FBI, the Nisei leaders of Watsonville's Citizens League (the name of the local JACL chapter) met and discussed the possibility of moving to Idaho. Word had reached Watsonville that there was a large apple

Students at San Juan Grammar School organize for a wartime scrap metal drive, May 1942. The Nisei students in this class were removed soon after the photograph was taken.

RUSSELL LEE, FARM SECURITY ADMINISTRATION

orchard for sale near Caldwell, Idaho, and after a lengthy discussion the community decided to form a farming cooperative and move as many people as wished to out to Idaho.

While a group of Nisei traveled to Idaho to investigate the property, the remainder remained in Watsonville preparing for the move. They scoured local junk yards and began assembling wagons and trailers from old automobile parts. A constitution was put together called the "Constitution of the Mesa Orchards Cooperative Farm Project." The Japanese community made two strong arguments for the move, the first of which was that it would enable the members of the community to move voluntarily out of Military Area #1. The second was that the community would be able to farm and assist in the national defense by producing food.

The Nisei who traveled to Idaho found several hundred acres of apple trees and a large amount of equipment, but they also found that the soil was extremely poor. Joe Moromoto, a veteran Watsonville apple packer, said, "The soil was nothing but rocks, and you could see the roots of the apple trees growing in and around them." The community met later in March to hear the report and sat in stunned silence as the young Nisei farmers told them of the poor soil at Mesa Orchards. Before they could find another property to examine, General De Witt closed Military Area #1 on March 29, 1942. The Watsonville community, and most of their fellow Japanese throughout the region, now waited to see what the government had in store for them.[14]

The San Benito County JACL went through a similar process but did not get as far along as their counterparts in Watsonville. Two Nisei, George Nishita and Henry Omoto, went to Salt Lake City to inspect some property near there, but they, too, found the property unsuitable.

Eventually, only 4,831 of the 114,222 persons of Japanese ancestry along the Pacific coast moved during March 1942, a testimony not only to the financial difficulty but also the fear of moving through the hostile interior of the United States.

LAST MINUTES PREPARATIONS

The first three months of 1942 saw a flurry of activity throughout the local Japanese communities. There was a surge of marriage licenses issued to local Japanese, as Nisei couples who had been thinking about marrying decided to do so and perhaps avoid being separated. Many Issei acquired birth certificates and proofs of birth for their Nisei children. Powers of attorney were arranged for the disposition of property and crops, and meetings were held to explain the intricacies of banking by mail.

Carrion-like buyers hovered around the edges of the community, buying things for pennies on the dollar. The inevitable evacuation sales of personal properties, boats, cars, homes, and businesses were followed by shopping expeditions to find sturdy and warm clothing. Since they did not know what climate awaited them, they bought clothing for every possibility.

WHAT ABOUT THE CROPS?

The government was extremely aware of the poor timing of this removal, as crops which the Japanese had so carefully planted in early 1942 were coming to maturity. An agent of the federal Farm Security Administration came into the region to assist in finding non-Japanese farmers to take over the fields being vacated. In early April, the special field agent for the FSA warned, "Tons of crops in the ground need immediate attention, and many acres will soon need planting, if we are to hold off a real agricultural disaster." He further noted that over half of the Japanese-operated farm acreage in Santa Cruz was still available for purchase or lease and that his office would assist anyone wishing to farm the land.[15]

Life magazine photograph documents the plowing under of the sugar beet crop because the Japanese had been removed, June 1942.   LIFE MAGAZINE

MEXICAN LABORERS TAKE THEIR PLACE

The agricultural crisis was averted by a special government program which encouraged the importation of temporary Mexican laborers to work the fields vacated by the Japanese. Mexicans began to arrive in the region in large numbers by the summer of 1942. This was the beginning of the bracero program, which saw thousands of temporary Mexican laborers in the California fields until the program ended in 1964.

TEMPORARY DETENTION CENTERS: SPRING-SUMMER, 1942

Despite their not having permanent camps ready for the Japanese who would be moved off the coast, the government decided to round up

Exclusion orders were posted until all persons of Japanese ancestry were removed from military area Number 1.   WAR RELOCATION AUTHORITY

all persons of Japanese ancestry and detain them temporarily in whatever facilities they could find. Had they waited a month or two, they could have used college campuses and dormitories which were designed for human occupation. Instead, they began in late March, using buildings which most recently had housed livestock.

Throughout this lamentable event, the government found it necessary to use euphemisms when describing the various stages of the incarceration. The phrase "Assembly Center" is most often used for this stage, but the implication is that the Japanese willingly assembled in them. They did not. They were unwillingly detained in these temporary facilities, and as such, the Japanese community now prefers to use "Temporary Detention Centers" when describing them. They were, in fact, prisons.

Most of the centers were fairgrounds or race tracks, places which were securable and relatively easy to convert into prisons.

EXCLUSION ORDERS

The first exclusion order, Exclusion Order #1, was issued on March 24, 1942, at Bainbridge Island, near Seattle. From that order until early summer of 1942, 106 other orders were issued throughout Military Area #1, the idea being that each order would involve approximately 1,000 people. Exclusion Order #15 applied to Monterey County, #16 to Santa Cruz County, and #77 to San Benito and Southern Santa Clara Counties.

WHAT THEY COULDN'T TAKE ALONG

The losses of real property, personal property, and businesses are always mentioned during any discussion about the relocation. However, one of the greatest losses suffered by many Japanese families was irreplaceable historical artifacts, mementos, and records. In some instances these belongings were destroyed in the early months of the war because Issei believed that merely having records and writings in Japanese was sufficient to bring in the FBI.

Priceless journals, personal papers, photographs, and documents went up in smoke as families hastily burned them. Gennosuke Kodani, for example, had kept a daily journal from his early days in the abalone industry in Japan in the 1890s up to his death in Monterey in 1930. Kodani's son, Seizo, at the urging of his mother, took the journals soon after December 7 and burned them behind the family home at Point Lobos. Scenes such as these were repeated

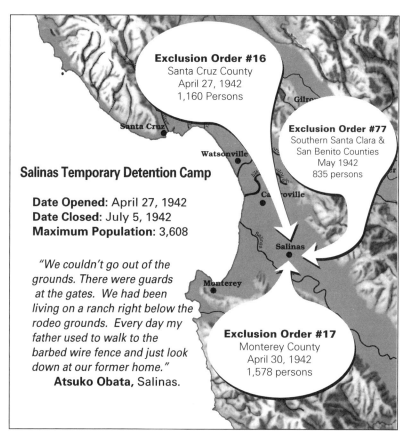

Exclusion Order #16
Santa Cruz County
April 27, 1942
1,160 Persons

Exclusion Order #77
Southern Santa Clara &
San Benito Counties
May 1942
835 persons

Salinas Temporary Detention Camp

Date Opened: April 27, 1942
Date Closed: July 5, 1942
Maximum Population: 3,608

"We couldn't go out of the grounds. There were guards at the gates. We had been living on a ranch right below the rodeo grounds. Every day my father used to walk to the barbed wire fence and just look down at our former home."
Atsuko Obata, Salinas.

Exclusion Order #17
Monterey County
April 30, 1942
1,578 persons

throughout the region until the Exclusion Orders finally went up in April 1942.

SALINAS TEMPORARY DETENTION CENTER: APRIL 27 - JULY 4, 1942

The reasons for using the Salinas Rodeo Grounds as a prison for detaining the Japanese instead of other fairgrounds in the region are not yet clear. One obvious advantage the facility had was that it was somewhat isolated on the north side of Salinas, and it was centrally located in the region. The perimeter of the grounds was quickly upgraded to contain humans. Guard towers were erected on the corners of

Internees and their personal belongings, Salinas, May 1942.
RUSSELL LEE, FARM SECURITY ADMINISTRATION

the property, and by late April 1942, the first groups of Japanese began to arrive.

LIFE AT THE RODEO GROUNDS

Most of the housing in the detention camp was in hastily built barracks made of green lumber. Cracks quickly appeared in walls and floors and the chill evening air came through with ease. As the number of people in the camp grew steadily through May, housing in the barracks became more and more crowded. Much of each day was spent waiting in long lines—for each meal and to use the meager shower facilities and latrines.

There were no flush toilets in the rodeo grounds. The open ditches which ran beneath the makeshift privies were filled with raw sewage, and the stench was unbearable.

Beyond the obvious unhappiness at being removed from home and business for no reason, perhaps the most difficult part of being in the detention camp was a distressing lack of personal privacy. Military-style gang showers and privies without partitions caused many internees to avoid those facilities whenever possible. Meals were also taken communally and the poor quality of the food was also noted by many of the internees.

But the Japanese made the best of a bad situation. A branch of the Monterey County Library was opened under the direction of Fusako Kodani, and at least one Salinas grammar school staged a drive to collect and donate magazines and books to the camp.

Life and death continued in camp with six births, two deaths, two marriages, and two divorces occurring during the first month the Japanese were there.

The temporary detention centers were administered by the WCCA or Wartime Civil Control Administration. The WCCA, appointed E. A. Rose as camp director and he and his fourteen fellow staff members administered departments ranging from police and fire to the camp kitchens and commissary. By mid-May a self-governing body was formed called the Center Council. Consisting of fourteen Japanese, this council met regularly to advise the camp administration of problems as well as pass directives on to camp residents.

Like any other prison, boredom was the greatest difficulty faced by most of the camp resi-

Japanese internees arriving at the Salinas Rodeo Grounds, April 1942. Some of the Japanese moved into hastily constructed barracks, while others moved directly into the horse stalls.

WAR RELOCATION AUTHORITY

dents, so the WCCA quickly helped organize athletic leagues in softball and sumo wrestling. The Buddhist and Christian churches continued to meet regularly.

A weekly camp newspaper named the "Village Crier" began publishing on May 11 and continued for eight issues until the camp was closed in July. An editorial in the second issue provides a good example of the values which helped the community through this difficult time:

> Discouragement, dissatisfaction and forlorn hope are to be felt when there is sudden change of pace in our normal existence. Many of us have left behind the fruits of years of hard labor and thoughtful planning.
>
> Belief and faith in the ultimate success that is our heritage will help us through this adjustment period. We are not lost! Be strong.
>
> We are 3,000 strong with physical features that are alike. Does that make us think or do the

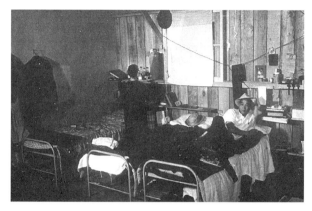

Akira Toya reclines on his bed in one of the new barracks at the Salinas rodeo grounds. Note the sheet placed over the window for privacy.
FARM SECURITY ADMINISTRATION

things identically as the next person? Surely, we have a mind of our own.

For the majority of us this is perhaps the first time in our lives that every little thing we do benefits the entire community. No matter how insignificant or great your service, it is you, the person next to you and next who shall reap the harvest of our endeavor.

Let's cooperate and be of service to all.

PREPARATION FOR ARIZONA

The Japanese community had known all along that their tenure in the rodeo grounds was temporary. In mid-June the WCCA announced that the inmates at Salinas would be moved to a camp in Arizona. On June 18 the WCCA staff held a party titled "Why Arizona?" for the camp residents, but many camp residents were concerned about just what Arizona might have in store for

Salinas Rodeo Grounds grandstands are in the center surrounded by barracks and stalls which housed over 3,500 internees.
WAR RELOCATION AUTHORITY

them. The most popular book in the camp library was a world atlas which contained one of the few maps of Arizona.

EFFECTS OF THE TEMPORARY DETENTION CAMP

A theme which runs through the accounts of most of the Japanese who spent time at Salinas was the unfairness of being arrested and the frustration of being so close to home yet so far away. As one Watsonville Nisei put it, "It didn't seem fair because they were supposed to send the Germans and Italians [to detention camps] too....but the government never did."[16]

One side effect of their stay in Salinas was that it provided a dress rehearsal for the permanent camps to follow. From the self-governing central committee to the recreational leagues, the Japanese community learned to work together, both with their own various regional communities and also with the camp staff and hierarchy. Through it all, though the adjust-

Aerial View of Poston Concentration Camp, where most of the Monterey Bay Region's Japanese were imprisoned in 1942.

WAR RELOCATION AUTHORITY

"Farewell"
Was this to be
Farewell?
A last, longing gaze
Thro' the infinite
Darkness
Toward the town,
My home —
One comfort:
Street lamps
Glistened thro' the
Mist
Like tear-filled
Eyes.

by Fuku Yokoyama
PUBLISHED IN "THE VILLAGE CRIER," JUNE 18, 1942.

ments must have been horrendous for many camp inmates, a sense of optimism and doggedness comes through. The weeks spent in Salinas helped the Japanese begin to acclimate to camp life, the loss of privacy, and the need to sublimate their individual needs to that of the group.

Salinas was a transition period, and without it, their removal to the Arizona desert could have been an unmitigated disaster. As it was, despite the Salinas experience, it was almost a disaster anyway.

CLOSING THE SALINAS TEMPORARY DETENTION CENTER

The camp was emptied beginning June 28, with 500 internees leaving each day. Everyone remembers the train ride from Salinas to Arizona. With curtains drawn, the Japanese rode into the San Joaquin Valley and then south, the temperature growing hotter and hotter by the hour. They could hear crowds of people shouting when the train stopped in Los Angeles, but

CAMP TIME-LINE

October 30, 1942 — Evacuation complete.

January 28, 1943 — War Department announces formation of all Japanese combat unit.

February 8, 1943 — Loyalty questionnaire administered in concentration camps.

May 1943 — The all-Japanese American 442nd Regimental Combat Team assembled in Mississippi for training.

January 20, 1944 — War Department extended draft to Nisei in concentration camps.

October 30, 1944 — The "Lost Battalion" from Texas rescued by the 442nd Regimental Combat Team in France.

December 18, 1944 — U.S. Supreme Court issued ruling that WRA cannot detain loyal citizens any longer.

September 2, 1945 — Japan surrendered.

September 4, 1945 — Public Proclamation #25 revoked exclusion order against persons of Japanese ancestry.

they were not allowed to look. Then the train turned east toward the desert camp that would be home for most of them for the next three years.

On July 4, Independence Day, the day that the Japanese in the region had celebrated with so much enthusiasm, they found themselves in another kind of parade, this time on their way to an unknown prison in the desert.

Poston Concentration Camp at night.   WAR RELOCATION AUTHORITY

CONCENTRATION CAMP: POSTON, ARIZONA

There has been an on going discussion since 1946 about just what to call the camps. The government used the euphemism of "relocation centers" to describe the ten camps set up to house the Japanese for the duration of the war. There was considerable reluctance within the Japanese community to use the term "concentration camp" because of the experiences of the Jews in similarly named camps in Europe during World War II. Over time, however, after extensive research determined that many of the government officials involved in setting up and administering the camps called them "concentration camps"—including Franklin Roosevelt, Harry Truman, and General Dwight Eisenhower—the Japanese community agreed to use the stronger term rather than the euphemism. The evolution of the nomenclature of the prisons reflects a similar evolution in the feeling of the

Japanese community about the camps.

INTO THE DESERT

The movement from summertime Salinas with its foggy, chilly evenings to the Arizona desert was extremely difficult. Every letter from Poston to friends and acquaintances back in the Monterey Bay Region contained references to the heat.

July 6, 1942 - Resident of Block 2. "I was very sick and tired ever since I came to this camp. The heat is so terrific that I won't be able to eat the food they give us and can't sleep until about midnight. Lost over 10 pounds and in bad shape now...110 degrees inside and 120 degrees outside, and the coolest we had was about 105 degrees inside...It's 0 miles from hell and I mean it."

July 9, 1942 - Resident, Block 2. "I have never in my life suffered as much as I have in this camp. Yesterday was one of the hottest days since we came here. The inside temperature was about 119 degrees and outside was over 123....I lost 12 pounds last week."

July 9, 1942 - Resident, Block 2. "It sure is hot here; it's like being in the middle of an oven. We were all surprised to find ourselves in the middle of a desert—nothing but sand and sagebrush. Nine people died already including a soldier who died with sunstroke....Everyone's getting heat rashes, bloody noses and fainting spells....When the dust storm comes, you can't even see the per-

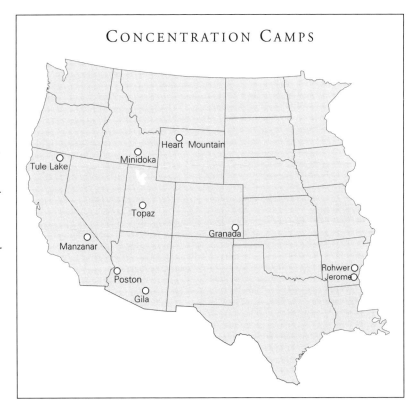

CONCENTRATION CAMPS

son next to you."

July 28, 1942 - Internee from Watsonville. "There's still some Watsonville pride. When the people from Salinas Center [the Rodeo Grounds] got here they started fainting left and right. Mostly people from Salinas California fainted. As a whole, Watsonville people were strong. One Watsonville man died, and seven Salinas people died."

August 1, 1942 - Resident, Block 2. "There is one thing the people are complaining about. That's the food we're eating. Compared to what we had in Salinas, the food is terrible....Fresh milk, fresh fruits and vegetables are very scarce. Many people are constantly losing weight because of the insufficient food and becoming lazy, cranky, hysterical and very selfish."

RESETTLEMENT LEAVE PROCESSES

Even before the last internees left the temporary detention centers, the government instituted a policy of allowing some Nisei to go on extended leaves outside the camps. By September 1945, over 30,000 Nisei had left the concentration camps on extended leaves.

LOYALTY AND THE QUESTIONNAIRE

In conjunction with the resettlement leaves, the government set out to accomplish what it said it couldn't do—determine the loyalty or disloyalty of individual members of the Japanese in the camps. In February of 1943 all internees over seventeen years of age were required to complete a thirty-question form which included questions about their family history, closest living relative in Japan, and foreign travel. Questions No. 27 and No. 28 became the cause for a controversy within the Japanese community which reverberated for years following the war. The questions as originally written:

The 442nd Regimental Combat Team fought valiantly against the German forces in Europe.   U. S. ARMY

No. 27. Are you willing to serve in the armed forces of the United States on combat duty, wherever ordered?

No. 28. Will you swear unqualified allegiance to the United States of American and faithfully defend the United States from any or all attack by foreign or domestic forces, and forswear any form of allegiance or obedience to the Japanese emperor, to any other foreign government, power or organization?

These were stupid questions. For Issei, to be asked if they would join the military was ludicrous. They knew they were not eligible for military service. This question had been intended for Nisei, but, by mistake, it was asked of everyone. "What was the government up to?" they wondered. Question No.

Nisei volunteers taking the oath as they joined the U.S. Army. Most Nisei chose to serve despite the fact that they and their families had been deprived of their personal liberties.
U.S. ARMY

SAN BENITO COUNTY BOARD OF SUPERVISORS RESOLUTION, APRIL 1, 1943

Be it resolved that we most vigorously and earnestly protest against the above proposed actions and each of them; that we convey this protest to the Secretary of War, to the War Relocation board, to our congressmen and senators to the President of the United States and to each Board of Supervisors of the State of California.

That we urge upon these authorities the following reasons, based upon an extensive experience with the Japanese, for more than 40 years, an intimate knowledge of their character, and our observation of what occurred on December 7, 1941, and immediately thereafter; (1) Following Pearl Harbor and for the defense of the West Coast against attack and sabotage the Army wisely moved the Japanese from the Pacific Coast. NOW TO PERMIT THEM TO RETURN TO THEIR FORMER HABITAT WOULD SUBJECT US AGAIN TO THE DANGER OF SERIOUS SABOTAGE AND DIFFICULTY IN DEFENDING OUR SHORE LINE IN THE EVENT OF ATTACK.

(2) DUE TO THE TEMPER OF THE AMERICAN PUBLIC SINCE THE DASTARDLY ATTACK AT PEARL HARBOR we feel that IT WOULD BE DETRIMENTAL TO THE BEST INTERESTS OF THE JAPANESE THEMSELVES TO ALLOW THEM TO RETURN FOR RESIDENCE ON THE WEST COAST, and that difficult additional policing problems would be presented thereby in effecting their safety.

(3) IT IS IMPOSSIBLE TO DISTINGUISH BETWEEN LOYAL AND DISLOYAL JAPANESE. We are in no position to judge the emotions of the Japanese inasmuch as they have maintained their own schools and religion, and in many cases, dual citizenship with their main allegiance to the Emperor of Japan.

(4) IF JAPANESE WERE ALLOWED TO RETURN TO THIS AREA WE COULD NOT EXPECT THE COOPERATION OF PRESENT AGRICULTURAL OR INDUSTRIAL LABORERS ALREADY ENGAGED IN THE WAR EFFORT IF THEY WERE CALLED UPON TO WORK WITH JAPANESE EVACUEES.

(5) TO ALLOW YOUNG JAPANESE TO LEAVE RELOCATION CAMPS FOR EDUCATIONAL PURPOSES IN OUR COLLEGES WOULD BE UNJUST AND INEQUITABLE AS IT AFFECTS OUR OWN AMERICAN BOYS WHO HAVE BEEN TAKEN OUT OF COLLEGE AND ARE SO LOYALLY SERVING THEIR COUNTRY in the armed forces to the detriment of their education and employment.

(6) IT IS THE OPINION of this Board that these Japanese should be contributing substantially to the war effort but we feel that it should be in areas removed from the Pacific Coast and by group movement UNDER FULL AND PROPERTY CONTROL AND SUPERVISION BY THE ARMY. IN NO EVENT SHOULD THEY BE DISBURSED THROUGHOUT THE COUNTRY WITHOUT PROPER PROVISION FOR ABSOLUTE SURVEILLANCE AND CONTROL.

BE IT FURTHER RESOLVED THAT THE JAPANESE, BOTH ALIEN AND AMERICAN BORN SHOULD BE RETAINED IN RELOCATION CENTERS FOR THE DURATION UNLESS THEY ARE PLACED UNDER DIRECT AND ABSOLUTE SUPERVISION AND FULL CONTROL OF ARMY AUTHORITY and engaged in the furtherance of our war effort.[17]

28 was the real problem, however. Since Issei were still not eligible for American citizenship (and would not be until 1952), to answer the question in the affirmative would technically render them stateless. Citizens of nowhere.

The furor caused by the questionnaire caused the government to re-draft both questions, but the damage was done. Yet, despite the questions and the confusion, almost 90% of the 78,000 internees over seventeen years of age who filled out the questionnaires did so in the affirmative. The War Relocation Authority then removed many of those now "disloyal" internees to the camp at Tule Lake, California. Those who answered questions 27 and 28 negatively became known as "No Nos."

For a community in which loyalty was a very important value, the questionnaire and resulting fallout were extremely painful. In a sense, the community had broken ranks over the questionnaire and raised some doubts about the loyalty of some of its members. Subsequent studies have shown that it was rarely loyalty that caused people to answer "No" to the two questions. Concerns about family members being separated and misunderstanding caused most of the negative answers.

Yet the very existence of the "No Nos" was troubling to the community leadership, and even after the camps closed in 1945, there was a stigma within the Japanese community about being a "No No."

NISEI WHO RESETTLED

Hundreds of Nisei from the regional Japanese community availed themselves of the resettlement process and left Poston for inland cities.

The Shikuma and Sakata families of Watsonville took advantage of resettlement, as did Seizo Kodani and his new bride Fumi Kodani. Ironically, the Nisei who resettled found themselves in some odd occupations. Seizo Kodani, considered to be such a threat as to be removed from the west coast, was a night-watchman in a munitions factory in Ohio. (!)

THE RIGHT TO SERVE

No loyal citizen of the United States should be denied the democratic right to exercise the responsibilities of citizenship, regardless of his ancestry....Americanism is not, and never was, a matter of race or ancestry. President Franklin Roosevelt, February 1, 1943.

In early 1943 the War Department decided to form an all-Japanese combat unit. Segregated units of African Americans and Filipinos already existed, with both these units led by white officers. The ill-conceived questionnaire noted above was designed, in part, to determine which Nisei would be willing to volunteer for military service. The army depended upon volunteers during 1943, but not enough Nisei came forward. So, in early 1944, the process of selective service was extended to include both Nisei men within

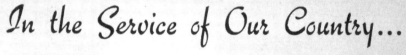

PFC. TED FUJIOKA
President of Associated Student Body, Spring, '43

ONE OF THE FIRST HEART MOUNTAIN
GRADUATES TO VOLUNTEER.
NOW OVERSEAS WITH THE ANTI-TANK
COMPANY OF THE 442ND COMBAT TEAM.

Nisei High School students at Heart Mountain honored the 442nd RCT members in their yearbook.

the camps as well as those who had resettled elsewhere in the United States.

Nisei men were taken out of the camps to go abroad and fight for the very freedoms that they did not have themselves.

THEY SHOULD STAY IN PRISON

Not everyone on the West Coast agreed with the government's resettlement and military service programs for Nisei. County Supervisor Peter Friis brought a resolution before the San Benito County Board of Supervisors, and though there is some confusion about the programs involved (there was no intent to relocate Nisei back to the West Coast), the Board unanimously approved the resolution on April 1, 1943.(For text of resolution, see p. 115.)

The climate of understanding which had been demonstrated in the early months of the war had been eroded away by April 1943 by

Daniel Inouye just before he lost an arm in Europe as a member of the 442nd RCT. Inouye is now the U.S. Senator from Hawaii. U. S. ARMY

the deaths of several San Benito county residents in the Pacific theater. When the concentration camps were closed in early 1945, San Benito County was an unwelcome place for the internees.

SELECTIVE SERVICE

As with the questionnaires, the vast majority of the Nisei reported for induction when ordered. Some, however, found the decision about whether to report or not to be very difficult. In the Heart Mountain concentration camp, for example, eventually eighty-five Nisei were tried and convicted of refusing induction. The Nisei at Heart Mountain stated that they had no obligation to service in the military as long as the liberty of their parents was denied.[18] In other words, it was loyalty to parents and to the United States Constitution which caused the Nisei at Heart Mountain to resist the draft.

What is important about these exceptions to the rule is that the Japanese community contained just as diverse opinions as any other community. The pressures of the camp experience brought many of those differences into bold relief.

It is not surprising that many young Nisei were extremely bitter after being removed from their homes and put into prison without due process of law.

THE 442ND REGIMENTAL COMBAT TEAM AND THE 100TH BATTALION.

The 100th Battalion was composed of mostly Hawaiian Nisei, while the 442nd was composed primarily of mainland Nisei. Other Nisei served in the Military Intelligence Service

(MIS), acting as Japanese language teachers, code-breakers, and translators.

Their combat record continues to be the most impressive of any units in the history of the United States military. A number of the region's Nisei became part of the 442nd Regimental Combat Team, and many were wounded or killed before war's end. Their contributions bore silent witness to the strong sense of loyalty felt by most of the Japanese, even those who were imprisoned.

There is no question that the exploits of the 442nd helped neutralize some of the racism that had been directed at the Japanese community. But, it did not negate that racism, as some Nisei in uniform were still barred from local services and facilities after the war ended.

Nisei veterans visiting the graves of comrades killed in action.

U. S. ARMY

CAMPS ARE CLOSED, 1945

In mid-December 1944, the Secretary of War sent a memo to President Franklin Roosevelt (just re-elected to an unprecedented fourth term in November) indicating that the "military necessity" of the camps no longer existed. Later that month the United States Supreme Court issued a ruling which paved the way for the closure of the camps, and beginning in early 1945, a few Japanese began to filter back to the West Coast.

The closure of the camps was as confusing as their opening, with many of the internees unsure of what was expected of them or where they might go. Some turned east to follow family members already settled elsewhere in the United States, but some set their sights for the Monterey Bay Region and home. In early 1945 a small trickle of Japanese Americans began to arrive in the Monterey Bay Region.

EFFECTS OF THE CAMPS ON THE REGIONAL COMMUNITY

The concentration camp experience was a watershed event for the community. Older

Memorial to those who died at the Manzanar concentration camp.

SANDY LYDON

members of the community still mark their lives as "Before Camp" or "After Camp."

COMMUNITY IS DISPERSED

World War II acted as a centrifuge on the Japanese community. Just the act of moving the community to camps elsewhere in the United States would certainly have resulted in some of the Japanese not returning, but when combined with military service and the resettlement programs, the effect on the regional Japanese communities was profound. By most community estimates, only one-third of the original Japanese residents of the region returned after the war.

Thus, in a very real sense, not only did individual community members have to start over after the war, but the communities themselves had to reorganize. For example, even though the Buddhist temples and Christian churches operated throughout the wartime evacuation, only a handful of pre-war members returned. Congregations of hundreds in 1940 shrank to dozens in 1945.

GENERATIONAL DIVISION

One of the greatest intergenerational disputes within the community occurred around the role of the Japanese American Citizens League. Since many of the Issei community leaders had been arrested early on and were still in detention centers throughout the United States, the leadership of the regional communities fell naturally to young Nisei and the JACL. In the weeks and months following December 7, the JACL had argued that cooperation with United States government authorities would be the best approach.

Once the camps were established, the JACL leaders found themselves to be targets of both angry Nisei and Issei, who felt that the organization was playing a collaborator's role. In fact, during the war, the JACL chapters stopped meeting and, in effect, disbanded.

Throughout the ten concentration camps, the only JACL chapter that continued to meet was the one from San Benito County. Meeting quietly and sometime beneath blankets to shield their meetings from view, the San Juan and Hollister Nisei met as much for social contact as for any political agenda. (After the war the San Benito County chapter of the JACL received an award from the national organization for its being the chapter with the longest, uninterrupted history in the United States.)[19]

ECONOMIC LOSSES

It is impossible to calculate with any precision the dollar losses suffered by the Japanese during World War II. But any analysis of this loss must include actual property lost, earnings lost during the war as well as future earnings lost.

One area where we can get some precision is that of real estate leasing and ownership. By taking the number of homes, businesses, and acres of agricultural land controlled by the Japanese in 1940 and comparing that with similar statistics in 1946, we might be able to get some idea of the magnitude of the losses. It must be noted, however, that there were many "off-the-record" arrangements between Issei farmers and non-Japanese landowners, ranging from cropping contracts to installment contracts done merely on a handshake.

The government was extremely interested in keeping agricultural land in production during the war. In the months following Pearl Harbor, the Farm Security Administration was charged with helping match non-Japanese farmers with Japanese farmlands. Once the Japanese were in camp, the War Relocation Authority set up an agency called the Evacuee Property Division, whose task was to "assist evacuees in the management and disposal of their properties."[20]

The greatest economic casualty for the Japanese during the war was the cancellation or reassignment of agricultural leases. As noted earlier, 70% of the land farmed by the Japanese prior to the war was leased, and with the assistance of the federal government, many of these leases were reassigned, renegotiated, or terminated.[21] Acreage owned by Japanese in camp also was sold to non-Japanese during the war. Land transfers occurred steadily throughout the war, reflecting not only the continued distrust which many Japanese had in their future, but also the result of the leave procedures and the

relocation of many Nisei into the interior of the United States.[22]

ECONOMIC NICHES LOST

The Japanese in the Monterey Bay Region lost outright several of the niches which they had developed prior to World War II. Perhaps the most serious break occurred in the fishing industry. While the Japanese were removed from the coast, the California legislature finally passed a law prohibiting Japanese nationals from acquiring commercial fishing licenses.[23] This meant that, when and if the Issei returned to Monterey, they could not resume either sardine fishing or abalone fishing. Not until a United States Supreme Court decision in 1948 (*Takahashi v. Fish and Game Commission*) held that California's license restrictions were uncon-

Poston concentration camp at sundown.

WAR RELOCATION AUTHORITY

stitutional, could Japanese nationals return to their boats.[24] By this time the Issei fishermen and divers were too old, and though there was talk of reviving the Japanese abalone business, it never happened.[25]

The other niche which the Japanese had dominated before the war was in intensive agriculture. While the Japanese farmers were away in camp, Euro-American farmers consolidated their holds on truck farming in both the Salinas and Pajaro Valleys, and the Japanese returned to an almost closed agricultural industry.

EMOTIONAL COSTS

Anger, resignation, or shame cannot be measured, but these may have been the highest costs of all for the Japanese community. The emotional responses to wartime removal within the Japanese community varied widely. There were some who were so angered by the actions of their government that they sought deportation to Japan. Others simply screwed up their determination to succeed and regain their losses once the war ended. But hovering over the entire episode was the sense of shame and the loss of personal honor. The Japanese community had been singled out and blamed for things that they did not do. For some the shame grew so strong that suicide was the only answer. There were a number of suicides in the concentration camps.

The focus of their shame often fell on the culture and traditions of Japan. Many believed that it was their "Japaneseness" that had brought relocation on the community, and many internees vowed to work even harder to adopt the culture of America. This feeling of shame about Japanese culture further widened the gap between the Issei and Nisei.

SUMMARY

World War II saw the regional Japanese community removed without justification or cause. The U.S. Supreme Court determined the executive order and relocation to be constitutional in decisions reached in 1943 and 1944, and though there have been a number of cases of individual Japanese overturned (Hirabayashi, Korematsu, and Yasui, most notably), the act continues to be legally constitutional.

The leadership of the Issei ended with the war. When most of the older community leaders were rounded up by the FBI and taken to detention centers in Montana and North Dakota, young Nisei found themselves thrust into leadership positions overnight.

World War II marked the end of the regional Japantowns. None of the Japantowns we have examined survived the war. When the Japanese returned they made very effort not to cluster businesses and homes as they had in the past.

Following the end of the war in 1945, the Japanese community returned to the region and attempted to pick up the pieces. But the community was (and is) also aware of the enormous precedent set by their being removed without benefit of trial or jury. The shame they felt about being singled out would, over the next half century, turn into a determination to see that it never happens to any citizen of the United States again.

Like the survivor of an unspeakable crime, the Japanese community has pondered for a half century whether or not it could have done more to prevent it. The answer always comes back—no.

The single word which is emblazoned across the accounts and memories of this period for the Japanese is honor. For them, it was, is, and always will be, a matter of honor.

7 SECOND BEGINNING
1945 to 1996

The postwar regional Japanese communities were very different from those that wartime removal obliterated. Each of the region's Japanese communities had a core of "old-timers," families who could trace their history in the region prior to the 1924 immigration exclusion. In most communities this older group was outnumbered by newcomers, Japanese who moved into the region from elsewhere along the Pacific Coast. Most of the Japanese living in the region in 1950 were from elsewhere in the state.

The reception the Japanese received in each of the region's communities varied widely. The Japanese encountered the most hostility in the region's agricultural valleys, where their competitors did not look forward to the resumption of competing with Japanese farmers. Salinas was the most anti-Japanese of the region's cities, with the issue of agricultural competition compounded by the large number of Salinas men who were killed in the Philippines early in the war. Unfortunately, the hatred many people in Salinas felt toward the now-defeated country of Japan spilled over onto the Japanese returning from concentration camps. The citizens of Salinas were still unable to disconnect the Japanese and

Seizo Kodani returned to Carmel after the war and eventually became the Chief of the Carmel Highlands Fire Department. KODANI FAMILY

Japanese American farmers who had lived and worked in the valley for almost half a century from the Imperial Japanese soldiers in the Philippines.

On the other end of the scale were the people on the Monterey Peninsula who took out an advertisement in the Monterey newspaper expressing their welcome and support for the returning Japanese.

The Japanese community organizations and churches attempted to resume business as usual, but it was a difficult task. The institutional and community histories written since the war have emphasized the common theme that the Japanese community has rebounded and "everyone lived happily ever after." Sadly, it has not been that simple. The internment experience has clouded the half-century of history since the war.

RETURN OF THE JAPANESE

As the camps began to close in early 1945, a few Japanese began to find their way back into the region. Some were Nisei working for the War Relocation Authority to assist in the community's return. The reception in each regional community varied from one of welcome as in Monterey to hostility and anger in Salinas and San Juan Bautista. Stories of "No Japs Wanted" signs are common to all areas, however, and confrontations over service in barber shops and gas stations seem universal throughout the region.

By all accounts, for the returning Japanese community, the Salinas Valley was the worst. Not only did the anti-Japanese stridency of organizations such as the Salinas Valley's Grower-Shipper Association continue to fill the air, but the situation was intensified by the story of the 194th Tank Battalion.

SHADOW OF BATAAN

Originally organized as a unit of the California National Guard, the small tank company was mobilized into the regular army and ordered into active duty in February 1941. As fate would have it, the 108 young Salinas men were on duty in the Philippine Islands when the Japanese attacked on December 8. Most of the unit members were captured by the Japanese army, and the story of their treatment both during the Bataan Death March and later as prisoners of war came back to Salinas and heightened the anti-Japanese sentiment already present in the community.

It was difficult for most Californians to separate the Japanese Americans from the Japanese

EMPTY HOUSE

I spent many childhood summers with my widowed grandmother who lived in a summer home in the Santa Cruz Mountains on the coast north of Santa Cruz. One summer not long after the end of the war, I remember riding in the family car as it wound through the coastal valleys covered at that time with fields of undulating blue-green flax. At the back of one of the flax fields was an old house, its windows long broken out. After several years of passing by this haunted-looking building, my curiosity got the best of me and I asked my parents about it. "Whose house was it? Why is it empty?" " A Japanese family lived there," they said." They grew strawberries in that field. They haven't come back yet," said my father. I remember wondering about the family and if they might return.

But each year the house continued to fall apart. The doors disappeared, then pieces of the walls, until finally, there was only a pile of old shingles to mark the spot. The Japanese family never returned.

SANDY LYDON

military in the Pacific, but in Salinas it was impossible. The fate of so many of Salinas' young men cast a red haze over everything that had anything to do with Japan. Even Japanese Americans.

SALINAS CHAMBER OF COMMERCE SURVEY, 1943

The effects of the decimation of the 194th Tank Battalion can be seen in a survey taken in

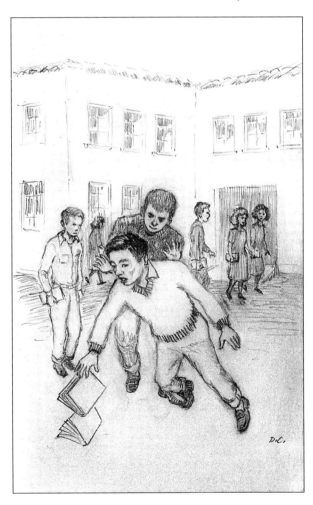

Duncan Chin remembers: "When the war was over, returning Japanese-American students had a difficult time at Watsonville High School. They were constantly being hassled by trouble makers. Their academic achievements, sports ability, and general friendliness eventually earned them the respect they deserved." DUNCAN CHIN

Salinas in 1943. Fred S. McCarger, the secretary of the Salinas Chamber of Commerce, was already on record in support of the removal of the Japanese. Fearing that the Japanese might be allowed to return to the coast before war's end, McCarger conducted a survey to gauge the public mood.[1]

The questions:

A. Do you believe it desirable that Japanese who are considered loyal to the United States be permitted to return to [the] Pacific Coast states during the war?
B. Does the opinion expressed in answer to question No. A represent the attitude of your family and those associated with you?

C. Is there any probability that [the] return of [the] Japanese would jeopardize their personal safety?

D. Would [their] return, in your opinion, involve dangers to your war operations?

E. Would their return cause resentment which would interrupt war production?

F. Is it desired that Japanese be permitted to return so that their labor may be utilized for: (a) Agriculture or (b) Industry?

G. How many persons does this vote definitely represent?

The results of the survey were astonishingly uniform. Of the hundreds who returned the survey, only one person answered question A in the affirmative. Totaling up the numbers in column G, over 1,400 people in Monterey County were represented, and save the one vote, all opposed the return of the Japanese to the coast.

SALINAS CHAMBER OF COMMERCE SURVEY, 1943

"We don't want [the Japanese] here at all. Remember Pearl Harbor.
"Keep [the Japanese] away from the Pacific Coast forever."
"We do not ever want them back."
"I wouldn't hire a Jap to work on my land regardless of how
bad labor is. In other words, we just don't want them
back here now or any other time."
"When the war is over send word to Japan to come get her Japs and keep them."
"They are out, keep them out forever. As a farmer [I] can get along very good without them."
"Send all Japs back to Japan—aliens and citizens alike—after the war."
"Please let me add that the only loyal Jap perhaps is a dead one."
"We hope that we never see another live Jap on the Pacific Coast."
"Take their franchise away and deport [every] last one of them."
"Confiscate all of their property, sell it to the highest bidder, [and] use the money received to help defray the cost
of defeating them."
"Once a Jap, always a Jap."[2]

All walks of life were represented in the poll, from agricultural laborers to the five county supervisors and their families. Bankers, accountants, lawyers, farmers, and businesspeople all voted against the return of the Japanese. The local chapter of the Daughters of the American Revolution, the American Legion Auxiliary, and various veterans organizations all voted against the Japanese. Local Parent Teachers Associations, school principals, doctors, and ministers cast their vote against the Japanese.

The survey is made even more powerful because of the individual comments that were collated along with the votes. Above is a sampling of the over 100 individual statements which respondents volunteered.

WHAT HAPPENED IN SALINAS?

After teaching, researching, and writing about anti-Asian racism in the United States for over thirty years, I considered myself beyond sur-

prise when it comes to the depths of American racism. I thought I had seen it all. But even the most strident anti-Chinese diatribes from the nineteenth century paled beside the results of this questionnaire. As I sat there reading the fading typewritten answers, the pure, unadulterated anger jumped off the page. The people saying these things were not Ku Klux Klan members from Alabama, they were the pillars of the Salinas Valley. They were the fathers and mothers of people I have known all of my life. As I turned the pages, I could only wonder about the conditions which would push people to say such things.

It seems to me that there are several possible causes:

ECONOMIC COMPETITION

An "understanding" had developed in Salinas between the farm owners and farm laborers—farm laborers should stay in the fields. The Japanese had moved up the agricultural ladder and challenged the grower leadership in the valley.

LEGACY OF VIOLENT STRIKES IN THE 1930S

The strike in September of 1936 brought violence to the city, with farm laborers pitted against machine-gun wielding growers. Though the Japanese were not directly involved, the growers no doubt believed that they were under attack on many levels.

RECENTLY ARRIVED "OKIES" FINDING A SCAPEGOAT

Old-time Salinas had abused the Okies in the late 1930s, and the war provided an opportunity for the white community to "close ranks," and turn and abuse the Japanese. Then, the capture of the tank battalion in early 1942 became the catalyst which brought all the other factors sharply into focus.

RETURN TO SAN BENITO COUNTY

Japanese who lived in San Benito County before the war still shake their heads when the subject of postwar San Juan Bautista comes up. The hostility which met them was similar to that found in Salinas. Anti-Japanese signs were posted on fence posts along the roads, and wherever they went, Japanese met verbal, and sometimes even physical, abuse. Some of the stridency can be traced to people suffering the loss of sons and daughters in the Pacific theater. Also, as in the Salinas Valley, the memory of competition with Japanese farmers was still very strong.

A temporary hostel was set up in the Japanese school building in San Juan and by September there were eleven families living there awaiting permanent housing in the valley. The War Relocation Authority was so concerned about the situation that they held a series of meetings in San Juan to discuss ways of diffusing the anti-Japanese feelings in the community. Along with pledges to assist the Japanese in finding housing, the WRA representatives counseled the Japanese to integrate into the local society. "Had you had such gatherings as these twenty years ago, evacuation itself might never have been necessary," said one WRA official.[3] The meeting concluded with the formation of the San Benito County Council for Civic Unity, which adopted as one of its principles: "It is un-American to penalize persons of Japanese descent in the US solely for the crimes of the government and military caste of Japan."[4]

The Council for Civic Unity seemed to have little impact on the situation. Three months later the WRA representatives returned, this time accompanied by combat veteran Lieutenant Colonel Wallace Moore. Moore made several personal appearances throughout the community, recounting the remarkable exploits of the Nisei in the military and exhorting the local populace to receive the returning Japanese back into the community. Moore declared that failing to serve Nisei soldiers in uniform was not only an insult to the U.S. Army, but it damaged the morale of those Japanese Americans still in uniform.[5]

Most of the prewar Japanese population did not return to San Benito County, and it took many years for the wartime conflicts to heal. The Japanese population of the county in 1950 was only 27% of what it had been in 1940.

JAPANESE POPULATION BY REGIONAL CITY, 1950

Monterey	531
Watsonville	321
Salinas	162
Santa Cruz	21

RETURN TO THE PAJARO VALLEY

The Chamber of Commerce and Agriculture of the Pajaro Valley conducted its own public opinion survey following the surrender of Japan in September 1945. Claiming to have surveyed a "broad cross-section of the business, agricultural, industrial and civic" segments of Watsonville and its surrounding area, the organization collated the returned surveys. The four survey questions are listed below with the majority responses:

1. Do you believe the return of Japanese may have harmful results, both to the Japanese and to our own citizens from a social standpoint? Responses: 3.5 to 1 in the affirmative.

2. Should local people employ or approve of the employment of Japanese evacuees? Responses: 4.5 to 1 in the negative.

3. Should former Japanese residents and their children be urged to re-settle in the Middle West? Responses: 5 to 1 in the affirmative.

4. Do you think property-owners would refuse to rent or sell land or houses to Japanese? Responses: 4.5 to 1 in the affirmative.[6]

Even though the survey was taken at the war's conclusion and there was no situation similar to the tank battalion in Salinas, the overwhelming sentiment in the Pajaro Valley was opposed to the return of the Japanese. The reception experienced by the returning Japanese in Watsonville varied widely. Some found their household goods and belongings had been carefully protected by Caucasian neighbors, while others found broken windows and empty storage spaces. Many early returnees spent their first days and weeks at the hostel set up at the Buddhist Temple on Union Street, and there were sporadic acts of vandalism directed at the temple.

The Izumizaki family's experiences in Watsonville in October 1945 were probably typical of most Japanese returnees. Kay and her daughter returned to the family home on October 1, while her husband Jimmy came back from serving with the 442nd RCT in mid-October. "Jimmy walked in the door on October 12, 1945; I remember it as clearly as if it were yesterday." In a recent interview Kay noted that the return was bittersweet: "It's funny. Many of the people we thought were our friends turned out not to be, and many who we didn't even know turned out to be the best friends we ever had."

And, despite the fact that Jimmy Izumizaki's brother, Henry, had been killed in action in Europe, he was not welcome in some places in Watsonville. In one classic instance, when Jimmy was refused service in a gas station, he sat in his car, telling the gas station attendant that he'd better call the police because he wasn't moving the car until he got gas. Jimmy eventually got his gasoline.[7]

RETURN TO THE STRAWBERRY FIELDS

The strawberry industry to which the Japanese returned was quite different from the one they had left in 1942. Because strawberries were not an essential wartime commodity, production dropped to zero acres during the war. So, not only did those Japanese wishing to resume strawberry farming have to regain their land (much of it had been leased prior to the war), but they also had to restart the industry from scratch. The Japanese also found that local Caucasian strawberry growers had taken advantage of the hiatus in production to develop and patent new strawberry hybrids. The Japanese strawberry growers not only had to start over but do so with a huge handicap.

RETURN TO SANTA CRUZ

Most of the Japanese living in and around Santa Cruz prior to World War II did not return at war's end. Not only did Santa Cruz continue its anti-Asian tradition that had begun in the nineteenth century, but the postwar economy of the area shifted farther away from agriculture to tourism and related industries. As the previous chart showed, there were only twenty-one persons of Japanese ancestry living in Santa Cruz in 1950.

RETURN TO MONTEREY

Monterey showed the most hospitality to returning Japanese of all the region's communities. In a remarkable full-page advertisement in the *Monterey Peninsula Herald* in May 1945, over four hundred Monterey Peninsula residents signed a pledge to extend "The Democratic Way of Life For All." Noting that many former Japanese residents of the peninsula might be returning to Monterey, the signatories agreed to "cooperate with the National Government by insuring the DEMOCRATIC WAY OF LIFE TO ALL MEMBERS OF THE COMMUNITY."[8]

Anti-Asian sentiment had always been minimal in Monterey, beginning with the anti-Chinese era of the 1870s. At that time, the reasons seemed to be that the Chinese were not competing directly with other groups in the community and that the multicultural nature of the town made mounting an anti-anything movement very difficult. In some ways, the Monterey of 1945 was not unlike that of the 1880s—only this time heavily influenced by southern European immigrants, particularly from Sicily. As we have seen, by the time Pearl Harbor was attacked in 1941, the Japanese fishermen had taken a minority role in the fishing industry. The only fishing niche completely dominated by the Japanese at that time was abalone diving. Thus, unlike the Japanese farmers in the Salinas and Pajaro Valleys who had achieved a very competitive and dominant economic position by 1941, the Japanese in Monterey had not.

A NEW-OLD MONTEREY NICHE: JAPANESE GARDENERS

Illustrative of the non-competitive relationship between the Japanese and the majority community in Monterey was the large number of Japanese gardeners working there both before and following the war. David Yamada notes that there were fifteen Issei- and Nisei-owned gardening businesses on the peninsula in the 1920s, and that the Japanese entered the business not only because it was open to them, but also because there were wealthy families on the peninsula needing the service.

Following their return to Monterey after the war, the Japanese gardeners resumed their dominant position in the gardening business and in 1955 formed the Monterey Peninsula Landscape Gardeners Association. Most of the founding members of the organization were of Japanese ancestry; but as the necessity for landscape gardeners shifted from the private estates to commercial accounts, such as hotels and motels, the dominance of the Japanese shifted until, in the 1990s, the MPLG had no Japanese members.[9]

IMMIGRATION RESUMES: MCCARRAN-WALTERS ACT, 1952

In an effort to reform and codify the diverse immigration laws on the books following World War II, Congress passed the Immigration and Nationality Act of 1952, over President Harry Truman's veto. (Truman objected to the law because it continued the discriminatory quota system.) The law marked several fundamental changes for the Japanese:

1. All races became eligible for naturalization. For the first time in United States history, Japanese were eligible to become naturalized citizens.
2. Japanese immigration resumed. Excluded since the 1924 Quota Act, Japanese immigrants were once again allowed to come to the United States. But, based on the mathematics still in place, Japan's annual quota was only 185 persons.

One might conclude that, with an annual quota of 185, there would not be many Japanese immigrants entering the United States following 1952, but the key element in the law was the right to become naturalized citizens. United States immigration law permitted citizens to petition for the immigration of their spouses on an unlimited non-quota basis. Thus, in a pattern not unlike that in the Gentleman's Agreement, between 1952 and 1965 a sizable number of Japanese women entered the country to join their husbands. In 1959, for example, 5,012 Japanese women entered the United States compared to 839 men.[10]

More Japanese came into the United States between 1952 and 1965 than any other Asian group. One of the primary forces behind this pattern was the postwar devastation and economic dislocation in Japan. And, as was the case prior to 1924, most of the new immigrants chose to come to California.

The result of this ever increasing number of women was that the Japanese community in the United States in

Fred Nitta, left, with his parents, celebrating their naturalization in 1953.

1965 was the only Asian group that had more female than male members.

REFUGEE RELIEF ACT, 1953

The Refugee Relief Act of 1953 permitted 214,00 aliens to enter the U.S. beyond the McCarran-Walter Act quotas. The law was aimed primarily at people escaping from Communist persecution as well as people fleeing natural calamities. The law expired in 1956.[11] Though most of the attention of this refugee act was focused on Eastern Europe, it also opened a small window through which came a

Harry Fukutome of Watsonville was one of the early post war immigrants from Kagoshima who helped pioneer the cut flower industry in the Monterey Bay Region.   SANDY LYDON

new group of Japanese immigrants into the Monterey Bay Region.

Since early in the century, the Japanese government had been encouraging Japanese nationals to settle in the colonial possessions of Korea and Taiwan and later in Manchuria. Following Japan's defeat in 1945, thousands of these colonists made their way back to Japan. The victory of the Chinese Communist Party in China in 1949 further intensified the flow of Japanese from Manchuria back to Japan.

When an organization in Japan learned that these refugees would qualify for emigration to the United States under the 1953 law, it set a goal to screen and find American sponsors for 1,000 potential emigrants to America.

FLOWER GROWERS

One new agricultural niche developed by the Japanese following the war was raising flowers in greenhouses. Pioneered by Nisei such as San Juan Bautista native, Roy Sakae, the industry eventually attracted a number of the new, refugee immigrants.

Unosuke Shikuma, a prominent member of the Watsonville Japanese community and member of the Westview Presbyterian Church, was the key figure in bringing the first new immigrants to the Monterey Bay Region. After visiting Japan in 1955 and interviewing some of the young men in Kagoshima and Yamaguchi Prefectures, Shikuma invited eight of them to come to the Pajaro Valley and work for him in the strawberry industry. After working for Shikuma for three years, the men could select their own occupations. One of the men, Akira Nagamine, went to the San Francisco Bay Area to learn the flower growing business by working in the carnation business there. Then, with

Shikuma's support and encouragement, Nagamine returned to the Pajaro Valley, where he began to grow carnations in greenhouses.

Cleaner air and cheaper land prices soon brought other flower growers from the Bay Area into the Monterey Bay Region, and greenhouses began to multiply across both the Pajaro Valley and the Salinas Valley.

Nagamine's brother, Osamu, and brother-in-law, Harry Fukutome, joined him and together they focused on learning all they could about the flower growing industry. Word of their initial success spread throughout the Japanese community, and a number of Kagoshima refugees came to the Pajaro and Salinas Valleys to start their own flower growing businesses. Growers such as the Nakashimas and Kitayamas joined the group, eventually organizing the Monterey Bay Flower Growers Association. At one point in the 1980s, over 90% of the flower growers in the Monterey Bay Region were Japanese who had immigrated to the United States after 1952.[12]

PREFERENCE PRIORITY IMMIGRATION REFORM, 1965

The civil rights mood of the 1960s spilled over into immigration reform in 1965, when Congress abolished the system that favored Western Europeans. The new preference priority system was based on the notion of reunifying families and providing equal access to all countries. Though the law was intended to assist previously restricted European families in unifying, the primary beneficiaries of the new system were Asian immigrants. It was as if all the pent-up pressures that had built since Chinese Exclusion in 1882 were finally unleashed.

The 1965 law had a limited effect on the Japanese community in the United States. One reason for this was that Japanese families in the United States were already intact by the mid-1960s, and there were few "reunifications" necessary. Secondly, and probably most importantly, Japan's economic progress made it increasingly undesirable for Japanese to leave. The "push" of eco-

Watsonville JACL leaders put up the sign for their new building on Blackburn Street in 1977.   BILL TAO

nomic dislocation that characterized Japan in the early twentieth century and immediately following World War II was not present in the 1970s and 1980s. Finally, some observers believe that wartime internment might have also tarnished the "sentimental idea" of life in the United States for Japanese immigrants.[13]

The Japanese community in America dropped from being the largest Asian group in 1965 to third, behind Chinese and Filipinos, in 1990. And, without a large influx of new immigrants, Japantowns in urban areas such as San Francisco and Los Angeles continued to shrink.

A DIVERSE REGIONAL JAPANESE COMMUNITY

By the 1970s, there were really three Japanese communities in the Monterey Bay Region. The first was the old-timers who had lived in the region before World War II and, despite the anti-Japanese hostility following the closing of the concentration camps in 1945, returned to rebuild their lives. The second was the new immigrants who had resided elsewhere in California prior to the war. These two communities had the shared experiences of alien land laws and wartime relocation in common. The third group was the immigrants who had come from Japan after 1952. These new immigrants had neither the prewar discrimination nor the wartime relocation experience, and the Japan they came from in the 1950s and 1960s was quite different from the one that the older Issei had left before 1924.

Over the years, most of the Nisei generation in the region had learned to take the conservative, less visible approach to solving problems.

The new immigrants, on the other hand, were much more outgoing in their approach and much more visionary and willing to take risks. As Mr. Sumio Koga noted in a recent interview, the new immigrants were "so alert and aware of the advantages America offered. They started more businesses around here...They see the opportunity in a bigger scope."[14]

The presence of these new, successful immigrants posed an educational challenge to the older community members who were convinced that the newcomers did not appreciate the price they paid to provide the opportunities of the 1950s and 1960s.

The greatest challenge came in the 1970s when the Sansei began to lead a campaign to reopen the issue of the wartime evacuation. It was one thing to get the surviving Issei to come forward with their stories and support the reopening of a terrible memory, but it was an entirely new challenge to educate a group of new immigrants about the importance of an event with which they had no personal experience.

BRINGING CLOSURE TO THE CONCENTRATION CAMPS

Looming behind the entire half century since the Japanese began returning to the Monterey Bay Region is the experience of evacuation and the concentration camps. It was a huge legal and moral wrong that needed some kind of closure.

It is difficult to measure the actual dollar losses of the Japanese community in the Monterey Bay Region. The wholesale termination of land leases in the agricultural valleys was compounded by the outright loss of land and homes. Evacuation sales in 1942 saw fishing boats, agricultural equipment, and personal property sold for pennies on the dollar. And then, how do you measure the losses in such industries as strawberry farming, where not only did the farmer lose his land but also came back four years behind in research and development? Professional careers were interrupted and businesses terminated. And beyond all this is the loss of morale where older Issei were just too demoralized to start over again.

And the losses were unevenly distributed throughout the community. Some Nisei who were able to move off the coast prior to De Witt's finally closing the area were able to do quite well in the interior of the United States.

The issue was further compounded by the cultural differences between the Japan-born Issei and their America-born children. Most of

Bon dancers, Monterey Fair Grounds, 1976. One of the longest-standing cultural events is the Buddhist celebration of the dead held each summer. For many years the Monterey community held their festival at the Monterey County Fair Grounds, but in recent years it has been moved to the Buddhist temple in Seaside.   SANDY LYDON

the Issei took the traditional Japanese view—evacuation was an unpleasantness not to be noticed. "Let it go," they said. "Don't mention it." Some of the Nisei agreed with their parents, but others, such as those who had resisted the draft and taken the position that the entire episode was illegal, immoral, and unconstitutional, felt that some kind of repayment from the government would be appropriate.

JAPANESE AMERICAN CLAIMS ACT, 1948

With the incredible feats of the 442nd RCT still ringing in their ears, Congress passed an act to balance the financial losses suffered by the Japanese community during World War II. Congress appropriated only $38 million to settle an estimated 23,000 claims requesting $131 million. The resulting settlements amounted to 10% of the amount asked for, based on the dollar value of the loss in 1941. The final claim was settled in 1965.

REDRESS

Emboldened by the civil rights movement of the 1960s and ethnic nationalism headed by leaders in the African American and Native American communities, young Japanese Americans began in the early 1970s to press for reopening the issue of compensation for the wartime evacuation. Though there are no statistical studies available to determine exactly what percentage of the community supported the movement, Roger Daniels estimated that about one-third of the community supported the movement, one-third opposed it, and one-third had no opinion.

Each of the regional JACLs had differing opinions about the movement, and even after

TELEPHONE CALLS.

Between 1988 and 1990 I was the host of a regular television show called "Backyard Adventures" on the local Fox affiliate. One evening, after broadcasting a segment on the history of the wartime evacuation of the Japanese, I was in the Salinas studio as the telephones began to ring. Over the next hour we received about a dozen telephone calls from viewers complaining about the program. One of the callers put it very simply: "Why are you glorifying the Japanese in that program? Sending them to camp was the best thing that ever happened to them. They couldn't be trusted then and can't be trusted now."

SANDY LYDON

the Commission on Wartime Relocation and Internment of Civilians (CWRIC) was formed in 1980, there was some reluctance on the part of older members of the community to press for redress.

A number of regional Japanese residents testified at the commission hearings, and in 1983 the commission issued its report in which it recommended:

1) A formal apology signed by the President.
2) Presidential pardons for those convicted of violations of the various laws surrounding evacuation.
3) A special educational foundation set up by Congress to illuminate and educate about the wartime evacuation.

Issei pioneers attending the dedication of the plaque at Salinas, 1984.
SANDY LYDON

4) A $20,000 payment to each surviving camp resident.

The only dissenting member of the Commission was then-Representative Dan Lungren of California. (At this writing, Dan Lungren is California's Attorney General.)

It took five years for the CWRIC's recommendations to pass both houses of the U.S. Congress.

CIVIL RIGHTS ACT, 1988

Since President Ronald Reagan had made it clear that he did not support the redress effort, the supporters of the measure needed to get a "veto-proof" two-thirds majority in both houses before bringing redress to a vote. Meanwhile a number of groups including the American Jewish Committee added their support to the measure. The bill finally passed the Senate in the summer of 1988 and arrived on President Reagan's desk where he signed it on August 10.

The bill did not contain funding for the $20,000 compensation, however, and it took another year before Congress found the money to begin repaying the camp survivors. The first checks were issued to the oldest Issei in late 1990, along with the official letters of apology signed by President George Bush.

SALINAS RODEO GROUNDS MONUMENT, 1984

One project which the regional community could generally agree upon was to place a commemorative plaque at the Salinas Rodeo Grounds. In February 1984 a partnership of the JACL chapters from Salinas, Monterey, San Benito County, Gilroy, and Watsonville sponsored a ceremony featuring Judge William Marutani, one of the members of the CWRIC.

CONTINUING ANTI-JAPANESE SENTIMENT

Meanwhile, the anti-Japanese sentiment that was fanned into flames by World War II never completely disappeared. What sympathy the American people may have felt for the Japanese following the dropping of the atomic bombs in 1945 quickly began to dissipate as Japan regained her economic feet and became one of America's major competitors in the 1970s.

Plaque installed by the regional Japanese communities in February 1984.   SANDY LYDON

By the early 1970s, as the Japanese automobile industry began making inroads into the United States' preeminence in the world automotive industry, anti-Japanese sentiments reappeared. In Phoenix, Arizona, a Chevrolet dealer warned the public: "Remember Pearl Harbor, when they tried to take your country from you. They are back with cheap imports to take your jobs, pensions and social security."[15]

In 1974, a survey sponsored by the Japanese government found that only 36% of Americans polled believed they could trust Japan. The survey concluded that the cause of this distrust was primarily economic.[16] Thus, where prior to World War II it was Japan's military power that disturbed many Americans, by the 1970s it was Japan's economic might.

And, as before, the spillover of this anti-Japanese sentiment splashed onto Japanese Americans. Once again, most Americans could not distinguish between the corporations in Japan and the Americans of Japanese ancestry who lived next door. In 1973, Edison Uno, a Japanese American political activist in San Francisco, received threatening telephone calls on a regular basis.

The national director of the JACL, David Ushio, said: "Once again, we believe Japanese-Americans are being made the scapegoats for what Japan does. We are a recognizable minority."[17]

MURDER OF VINCENT CHIN, 1982

One of the most celebrated cases demonstrating the depth of anti-Japanese feeling occurred on the night of June 19, 1982, when Vincent Chin, a Chinese American, entered a bar in Highland Park just outside Detroit, Michigan. Chin, twenty-seven, went to the bar with several friends to celebrate his coming marriage, but once inside he was met with racial slurs and taunts from several unemployed automobile workers who mistakenly thought Chin was Japanese. Later that evening the auto workers trapped Chin in front of a McDonald's restaurant and beat him severely with a baseball bat. Chin died four days later. As Professor Ronald Takaki noted at the time, Chin's death was particularly poignant—in front of the Golden Arches, with the symbol of the national pastime, by men who did not take the time to find out whether Chin was Japanese or Chinese.

The murderers were initially allowed to plea-bargain the charges down to fines and probation, but the Asian American community rose in outrage. A federal investigation eventually resulted in a second trial, this time for depriving Chin of his civil rights, resulting in an aquittal. In a later civil suit a jury awarded $1.5 million to Chin's estate, but no funds were ever paid. Finally, in September 1987, Vincent Chin's mother moved back to China.[18]

The Vincent Chin case became a symbol of the intensity of anti-Japanese sentiment loose in the United States in the 1980s.

CURRENT TRENDS

The tendency in most local and regional histories is to declare that the Japanese have "returned to normal" since their removal during World War II. (This is an interesting variation on the "model minority" theme, which often sets up divisive comparisons between

them and other groups in the United States.) There is an almost urgent desire to paint a "happy face" on the present and future of the various Japanese communities in the region. And there is no question that the success stories certainly outnumber the failures. Area high schools have seen many Sansei and Yonsei valedictorians over the years since World War II.

Beneath the obvious successes, however, community leaders will reluctantly admit to being troubled by a number of trends:

1) The disappearance of traditional Japanese culture. The Issei had been the repositories of traditional Japanese culture, but with so few still living, the duty of transmitting Japanese culture has fallen to the Nisei. For many Nisei, Japanese culture had been the very thing that singled them out in 1942. Older Nisei who had reluctantly endured Japanese school now encourage their Sansei children and Yonsei grandchildren to learn as much about Japan as possible. But traditional Japanese culture is undergoing rapid changes in Japan also, and the pre-1924 Japanese culture of the Issei no longer exists anywhere. The older Japanese in the region find themselves standing on a cultural island made of sand, with the currents of the 1990s eroding it away on all sides. True, the art forms of bonsai and ikebana survive, but many younger Sansei and Yonsei don't really care for any of it.

2) The disappearance of Japanese ethnicity. Without the Nihonmachis and sizable immigration from Japan to anchor them, the Sansei are not only dispersed geographically throughout the region but are also marrying non-Japanese at a high rate. Most studies indicate that, statewide, over half of the Sansei have married non-Japanese and the rate continues to rise.[19] The children resulting from such marriages are known as "hapa," a word borrowed

from the Hawaiian phrase, "hapa-haole," meaning half white. No statistics are available on how many hapa children there are in the Yonsei generation, but I am seeing more and more of them in my classes at Cabrillo College. And, much like their Nisei grandparents, these hapa youngsters are working through the difficulties of feeling pulled by two cultures.

The story behind each of these out-marriages has a similar structure: Nisei parents (and Issei grandparents, if still living) did not approve of the romantic involvement with a non-Japanese, but once they "got to know them," they were accepted into the family.

CONCLUSIONS

Only a century has passed since the first Japanese immigrants entered the Monterey Bay Region and yet, it somehow seems much longer. Much like the traditional "shukkei" garden, where broad Japanese landscapes were scaled down and represented in miniature, the history of the Japanese in the region is compact and intense—compressed history. One obvious reason for this is that there are actually two histories—before and after World War II. The story has two "beginnings," a fact which makes it seem much more dense than the stories of other immigrant groups in the region. In earlier sections of this work I compared the early Japanese immigrant groups with their counterparts from China, noting the similarities and differences between the two groups. We might call this the more traditional way of looking at Asian immigration.

But as we stand here in the late 1990s, one of the striking things about the story is how perfectly balanced the pre- and postwar halves of the story are. Beyond their similar half-cen-

tury length, each seems to have similar characteristics. An analysis of the two halves illuminates some themes common to both and suggests some universals about both the region and the Japanese community.

NICHE-CARVING

The most obvious theme common to both periods was the need for the community to find and develop economic niches. The niches provided not only immediate economic support but also allowed the Japanese to set up wider group-oriented infrastructures. Only two of the niches survived the chasm of the war—farming and landscape gardening—and both were fundamentally changed in the process. It is difficult to know whether the outside pressures forcing the Japanese (and indeed other groups) into certain professions were stronger than the internal forces pulling them together, but it can be argued that there is something useful about being identified with a particular profession. It can also be terribly confining and restrictive, particularly to succeeding generations who wish to create their own identities.

SERVICE COMMUNITIES

Japantowns may have been dispersed by the war, but they continue to exist. The services provided to the Japanese community by prewar Nihon machis continue to be provided by Japanese-owned businesses, the only difference being that those businesses are no longer clustered together. Though it is not overtly stated, there is a network of businesses and professionals having predominantly Japanese clients. Older Japanese Americans in particular may find it more comfortable to go to a Japanese doctor or attorney. Again, as with the economic niches, how much of this is the result of overt discrimination against Japanese by non-Japanese businesspeople and how much of it is a centripetal attraction is difficult to measure.

IMPORTANCE OF CHURCHES AND TEMPLES

The region's Japanese temples and churches were formed in the very early years of the century and they continue to be the locus of community activities in the 1990s. And, just as the Issei lamented the diminishing membership in those churches in the 1930s, the Nisei now decry the declining numbers in the 1990s. But membership numbers do not tell the whole story. Whether it be teriyaki chicken dinners or Bon dances, the events sponsored by the regional churches and temples continue to be the public beacons of the Japanese community. The religious organizations took over the prewar role played by the Japanese associations, and most Japanese living in the region today have been on the grounds of one of the local temples or churches, even if they are not official members.

PERSISTENCE OF PUBLIC JAPANESE CULTURE

The Japanese Tea House in Pacific Grove was very popular with the public even in the midst of the anti-Japanese movement leading up the Alien Land Law of 1913. Traditional Japanese art (called "curios" at the turn of the century) was also extremely popular and continues to be in the 1990s. Flower arranging and bonsai growing have many established groups in the region. Membership in these organizations as well as the dance instruction preceding the Bon dances in the summer is open to non-Japanese,

and all forms of traditional Japanese artistic tradition have large followings outside the Japanese community. The use of traditional Japanese art forms to diffuse anti-Japanese racism and educate the general public about the Japanese community may not be overt and intentional, but the results are positive nonetheless. The fact that most of the art forms (the martial arts are the exception) are non-threatening and peaceful in their nature assists in disarming preconceptions about Japanese culture.

IMPORTANCE OF NON-JAPANESE ALLIANCES

During the days of the alien land laws it was essential for Japanese farmers in the region to forge partnerships (both official and unofficial) with European Americans, and that theme continued after the war. Perhaps the most prominent example of this was the formation of the agricultural conglomerate of Tanimura and Antle in Salinas. The reasons for these alliances may be different in the 1990s from those in the 1920s, but one of the common elements to the story is anti-Japanese sentiment which lurks continually in the background.

SUPPORT FOR COMMUNITY PROJECTS

The Japanese community has always been a major contributor in supporting public projects in the Monterey Bay Region. From their unstinting and quick donations to Liberty Loan and Red Cross Drives in World War I through their support for hospitals and other public institutions after the war, the Japanese often contributed in amounts well beyond the size of their community.

PRESENCE OF ANTI-JAPANESE RACISM

The specter of anti-Japanese racism continues to haunt the Japanese. Whether a recent immigrant, visiting student, or third generation America-born, most people of Japanese ancestry living in the Monterey Bay Region have experienced some form of racism. From the slur to outright discrimination in employment or housing, the virus of racism continues to live in the region, ready to burst forth at the slightest provocation. Where the Japanese associations worked to educate the public in the 1920s and 1930s about Japanese culture, the regional JACL chapters now work on teaching tolerance. But, despite their best efforts, anti-Japanese prejudice and discrimination are still very much a part of the landscape of the Monterey Bay Region. I have heard Sansei students remark that they would sometimes prefer to deal with the kind of overt, public racism that their grandparents suffered, as it would be easier to combat with the legal tools available in the 1990s.

IMPRINT OF THE JAPANESE

The Japanese have enriched the Monterey Bay Region in many ways. From the agricultural heartland they helped diversify to the maritime industries they pioneered, the Japanese made—and continue to make—their mark on the region. However, just like their Chinese predecessors, you will find very few landmarks or place names commemorating Japanese contributions. Some of that is the result of their traditional reluctance to boast, and some is the lingering resentment from World War II.

But I think it can be argued that their amazing story itself is their greatest legacy. Much can be learned from what the Japanese have done and how they did it. Some of the lessons are obvious—the importance of hard work, patience, family, and persistence. But the Japanese also have taught us a lot about honor. From the simple respect paid to community elders to the complex love of the country that forgot its own principles, the Japanese have kept their moral compasses aligned toward the most important ideals.

APPENDIX

APPENDIX A

JAPANESE IMMIGRATION TO THE UNITED STATES

1635 to 1885 - Japanese emigration not permitted by Japanese government. No restrictions on Japanese immigration by United States government.

1882 - Chinese laborers excluded from coming to the United States. Created need for labor, particularly in California.

1885 - Emigration legalized by Meiji government in Japan.

1900 - Japan stopped issuing passports to laborers to the United States mainland. Laborers continued to go to Hawaii and then to mainland United States

1907 - United States government stopped aliens from entering the United States mainland from Hawaii or Mexico.

1907/8 - Gentleman's Agreement. Japan agreed to issue passports only to laborers who had already been in the United States and to family members of emigrants already there. Opened the way for "picture brides."

1920 - Japanese government voluntarily stopped issuing passports to picture brides. Immigration declined each year from 1921 to 1924.

1924 - United States government excluded Japanese in Quota Act. Because Japanese were "aliens ineligible for citizenship," they had no quota. Angry response in Japan.

1952 - McCarran-Walter Immigration Act gave Japan a quota of 185 per year.

1968 - Preference Priority system began. Japanese immigrants no longer restricted by quotas.

APPENDIX B

JAPANESE IMMIGRANTS AND UNITED STATES CITIZENSHIP

1790 - Congress limited naturalization to "free white person."

1790 - Children born on United States soil are automatically United States citizens.

1870 - Congress added "aliens of African nativity and persons of African descent" to list of those eligible to naturalize.

1882 - Chinese Exclusion Act stated that Chinese were specifically not eligible for naturalization. Some confusion about exactly where the immigrants from Japan fit in the "free, white" definition. About 400 Issei naturalized at various locations in the United States.

1906 - Naturalization law reemphasized that whites and blacks were the only ones eligible to become naturalized citizens.

1922 - *Takao Ozawa v. the United States.* Ozawa lost his challenge to become naturalized. Japanese are declared ineligible for naturalization.

1952 - McCarran-Walter Act declared Japanese eligible to naturalize.

APPENDIX C

REGIONAL POPULATION OF CHINESE AND JAPANESE, 1880-1990

	1880	1890	1900	1910	1920	1930
MONTEREY CO.						
Total population	11,302	18,637	19,380	24,146	27,980	42,646
Japanese	0	1	710	1,121	1,614	2,271
Chinese	372	1,667	857	575	748	613
SAN BENITO CO.						
Total population	5,584	6,412	6,633	8,041	8,995	11,311
Japanese	0	0	15	286	427	559
Chinese	242	85	69	66	104	9
SANTA CRUZ CO.						
Total population	12,802	19,270	21,512	26,140	26,269	37,433
Japanese	0	29	235	689	1,019	1,407
Chinese	523	785	614	194	215	238
TOTALS REGION						
Total Population	29,688	44,319	47,525	58,327	63,244	91,390
Total Japanese	0	30	960	2,096	3,060	4,237
Total Chinese	1,137	2,537	1,540	835	1,067	860

1940	1950	1960	1970	1980	1990
73,032	130,498	198,351	250,071	290,444	355,660
2,247	1,564	3,173	3,246	3,828	4,196
589	713	1,080	1,345	1,590	2,165
11,392	14,370	15,396	18,226	25,005	36,697
526	142	186	111	142	184
9	33	71	34	33	52
45,057	66,534	84,219	123,790	188,141	229,734
1,301	848	1,163	1,430	1,830	2,310
363	384	412	607	830	1,633
129,481	211,402	297,966	392,087	503,590	622,091
4,074	2,554	4,522	4,787	5,800	6,690
961	1,130	1,563	1,986	2,453	3,850

APPENDIX D

UNITED STATES IMMIGRATION LAW

With immigration such a controversial issue in California in the 1990s, it is essential that all Californians have an understanding of the history and current status of immigration, citizenship, and marriage laws as they pertain to immigrants to the United States from Asia. The following summaries are only the highlights of a century's worth of extremely complex legislation. This list is not meant to be definitive.

The legal authority to regulate immigration into the United States rests with the United States Congress. Though there have been many efforts by states and local jurisdictions to get into the "immigration regulation business" (California's Proposition 187 in 1994, as an example), the United States Supreme Court has consistently found that immigration regulation is the prerogative of the federal government in general and Congress in particular.

PHASE ONE: UNRESTRICTED IMMIGRATION, 1776 TO 1875

During this period there was no federal legislation in place regulating immigration. Several states attempted to do so (including New York, Massachusetts, Louisiana, and California) by placing taxes on immigrants, but all state laws were struck down by the United States Supreme Court. Several efforts to restrict the large Irish-Catholic immigration in the 1840s were made in Congress, but they failed to pass.

PHASE TWO: INCREMENTAL RESTRICTIONS, 1875 TO 1921

Responding to increasing immigration from Southern and Eastern Europe and Asia, Congress tried to change in a piecemeal fashion the profile of the American immigrant. Sometimes responding to regional concerns and sometimes responding to international events, these laws reflect the times in which they were passed rather than any grand scheme to control and shape immigration.

1875 - The Page Law. Prohibited the importation of women for purposes of prostitution. Directed specifically at Chinese women, this was the first federal regulation of immigration. Enforcement of the law was overzealous, particularly in California ports. Many Chinese women who were not prostitutes were excluded, leading to the erroneous belief that a law had been passed prohibiting the immigration of Chinese women.

1882 - Chinese Exclusion Act. Chinese laborers were prohibited for ten years, but scholars, students, and merchants could immigrate. Since Chinese women were defined as laborers, this law effectively stopped the immigration of Chinese women and prevented the formation of Chinese families in the United States.

1882 - Qualitative limitations. Congress also added lunatics, idiots, and people unable to support themselves as prohibited immigrants. A tax of fifty cents was also placed on each legal immigrant to the United States to help pay for processing.

1885 - Contract laborers prohibited. In response to several economic downturns in the 1870s and 1880s, Congress passed a series of laws excluding immigrants coming to the United States under contracts that required them to work for an employer for a particular length of time.

1888 - Scott Act. All Chinese laborers outside the United States, including those who were in the United States prior to 1882, were prohibited from returning. This act caught many Chinese who had returned temporarily to China with legal return certificates.

1891 - More qualitative limitations. Congress excluded persons suffering with "loathsome or contagious diseases," felons, and polygamists.

1892 - Geary Act. Besides renewing Chinese exclusion for another ten years, the Geary Act required all Chinese laborers in the United States to carry a federal registration certificate. After the Supreme Court upheld the constitutionality of the law, the majority of Chinese in the United States complied with it.

1902 - Renewal of Chinese exclusion. Congress renewed for another ten years the exclusion of Chinese laborers.

1904 - Chinese exclusion made permanent. Congress extended Chinese exclusion indefinitely.

1908 - Japanese laborers excluded. Because Japan was a major military power, the United States had to resort to cautious diplomacy to control Japanese immigration. In the resulting agreement—known as the Gentleman's Agreement—Japan agreed to stop issuing passports to laborers headed for the United States. Japanese wives and children could continue to come to the United States, as well as Japanese laborers who had already immigrated.

1917 - Illiterate adults excluded. The Immigration Act of 1917 codified all previous restrictions and included a literacy requirement. All immigrants over sixteen years of age had to be able to read. This law was passed over President Wilson's veto. The laws also created the "barred zone," whose immigrants were declared inadmissible. The zone included part of China and all of India and Southeast Asia.

1918 - Alien anarchists excluded. Aliens who believed in or advocated the overthrow of the government were excluded. This was in response to the 1917 Bolshevik revolution in Russia and the growth of Communism in the United States.

PHASE THREE: CONTROL OF QUANTITY AND COUNTRY OF ORIGIN, 1921 TO 1965

Up to 1921 there had been no numerical limitations on immigration to the United States, but following World War I, rising antiforeign sentiment in the United States began to demand not only a limit as to the number of immigrants but also restrictions on immigrants from "less desirable" countries.

1921 - The First Quota Law. This law was a major departure from previous immigration policy. The law limited immigration to 3% of the number of any nationality living in the United States in 1910 and put a ceiling of approximately 350,000 immigrants a year. The law favored immigrants from Northern and Western Europe. Nations in the "barred zone" had no quotas.

1924 - National Origins Quota System. (Also known commonly as the 1924 Quota Act.) This law refined and made permanent the provision in the 1921 law. The biggest addition to the law was the provision that aliens ineligible to citizenship would have no quotas.

QUOTAS FOR PERIOD 1924 TO 1929

For the first five years the quotas were based on 2% of the number of nationals living in the United States in 1890. The minimum for quota countries was set at 100 per year. The annual total of immigrants for this period was 164,000.

Some selected annual quotas:

Germany	51,227
Great Britain	34,007
Ireland	28,567
Sweden	9,561
Norway	6,453
Poland	5,982
France	3,954
Italy	3,845
Czechoslovakia	3,073
Denmark	2,789
Russia	2,248
Switzerland	2,081
Netherlands	2,648
Yugoslavia	671
Portugal	503
Spain	131
Greece	100
China	0
Japan	0

QUOTAS FOR PERIOD 1929 TO 1952

In 1929 the basis for the law shifted to the percentage of that nationality in the United States in 1920 taken against a total of 150,000. For example, if a group comprised 10% in 1920, that group would have an annual quota after 1929 of 15,000. No group had a quota of less than 100, so the base annual immigration total was 154,277. Groups whose immigrants were ineligible for citizenship continued to have no immigration quota.

Selected annual quotas for this period:

Great Britain	65,721
Germany	25,957
Ireland	17,853
Poland	6,524
Italy	5,802
Sweden	3,314
Netherlands	3,153
France	3,086
Czechoslovakia	2,874
Russia	2,784
Norway	2,377
Switzerland	1,707
Denmark	1,181
Yugoslavia	845
Portugal	440
Spain	252
India	100
China	0
Japan	0

1934 - Philippine Independence Act gives the Philippines an annual immigration quota of 50. Heretofore, Filipinos had been able to move freely from the American-controlled Philippine Islands to the mainland of the United States.

1943 - Repeal of Chinese Exclusion. As a result of China's being an ally of the United States in the war against Japan, the Chinese Exclusion Laws were repealed and China was given a special annual quota of 105 persons each year.

1946 - India and Philippines given annual quotas of 100.

1952 - McCarran-Walter Immigration Act. Passed over President Truman's veto (he felt that the quotas were discriminatory), the law continued the National Origins Act quotas, which had been in place since 1929, along with a major change:

All nationalities and races eligible for citizenship. This gave countries who had no quota because their immigrants were "ineligible for citizenship" immigration quotas for the first time. Japan, for example, now had a quota of 185.

PHASE FOUR: PREFERENCE PRIORITY SYSTEM, 1965 TO PRESENT

After considerable study, Congress enacted an entirely new system in 1965, which took effect in 1968. Implemented during the national debates on civil rights, Congress put in a new system based on preference priorities. The relatives of citizens and residents already in the United States were given priority as were professionals and refugees. The Eastern Hemisphere was limited to 170,000 quota immigrants per year (immediate family members were beyond the total quotas). The preference priority categories:

First preference: Adult unmarried sons and daughters of United States citizens.
Second preference: Spouses and unmarried sons and daughters of lawful permanent resident aliens.
Third preference: Professionals and those with exceptional abilities in the sciences or the arts.
Fourth preference: Married sons and daughters of United States citizens.
Fifth preference: Brothers and sisters of adult United

States citizens.

Sixth preference: Skilled or unskilled workers.

Seventh preference: Refugees from either Communist dominated countries or natural catastrophes.

The expectation of Congress in 1965 was that the system would benefit primarily southern and eastern European immigrants. But they had not been paying much attention to developments within the Asian American communities. What happened after 1965 caught them by surprise. Asian families moved quickly to put themselves back together; women joined their spouses. Asian countries used preferences two and five as their primary means of immigrating to the United States. The result was an upsurge of Asian and Latin American immigration since 1970, with an attendant decline of immigration from Europe.

1986 - Immigration Reform and Control Act. Gave illegal aliens amnesty and instituted sanctions for employers who hired illegal aliens.

1990 - Immigration Reform. Increased total immigration from 500,000 to 700,000 annually, with permanent leveling off at 675,000. Law was a general effort to encourage European immigration which was restricted by having no family members already in the United States. Immediate relatives (children, spouses, parents) of United States citizens would be limited to 520,000 visas per year.

APPENDIX E

CITIZENSHIP - WHO CAN BECOME A CITIZEN?

Basic Authority: The United States Congress has the authority to determine the qualifications for becoming an American citizen.

Citizenship by Birth: According to legislation passed in 1790, anyone born in the United States is a United States citizen. There have been minor modifications, but this has been and continues to be the law. The legal principle is known as jus soli, or the law of the soil.

Citizenship Through Naturalization: The process of changing from an alien into a citizen is known as naturalization.

1790 - Free and White. The basic naturalization law was designed to exclude slaves, Indians, and anyone else not white. There were numerous legal questions raised as to the definition of "white" over the years.

1870 - Free, White, and African Ancestry. Following the Civil War, Congress extended naturalization to ex-slaves, but specifically denied the Chinese the right because they had "undesirable qualities."

1882 - Chinese Exclusion Law reaffirms that Chinese are not eligible for naturalization.

1943 - Chinese eligible to become naturalized citizens.

1946 - Asian Indians and Filipinos added to those eligible to become naturalized United States citizens.

1952 - All national and racial barriers to citizenship removed in McCarran-Walter Act. Removed the phrase "aliens ineligible to citizenship."

REQUIREMENTS FOR BECOMING A UNITED STATES CITIZEN - 1996

1) Must be at least 18 years old.

2) Must be a lawful resident of the United States for 5 years prior to application.

3) Must demonstrate an ability to read, write, and speak simple English. (People over 50 who have been here for at least 20 years are exempt.)

4) Must be of good moral character.
5) Must not have been a member of the Communist party for at least ten years.
6) Must forswear allegiance to foreign country.
7) Must demonstrate a knowledge and understanding of the United States Constitution and American history and government.

LOSING YOUR CITIZENSHIP - WOMEN WHO MARRIED ALIENS

For a period of 45 years, some women who were citizens of the United States LOST their citizenship if they married aliens.

1907 - Marry a foreigner; lose your citizenship. Any woman who was a United States citizen who married an alien "shall take the nationality of her husband." This law applied to all marriages, not just those with Asian men.

1922 - The Cable Act. Amended the 1907 law by requiring the woman to overtly renounce her citizenship before losing it. But, the law also indicated that any woman who was a United States citizen who married an "alien ineligible to citizenship shall cease to be a citizen of the United States...." Thus, America-born Chinese and Japanese women who married immigrants from China or Japan lost their citizenship.

1952 - McCarran-Walter Act ends the Cable Act provisions.

Thus, from 1907 through 1943, American-born Chinese women who married Chinese immigrants lost their citizenship. From 1907 through 1952, American-born Japanese women who married Japanese immigrants lost their citizenship.

APPENDIX F

WHO CAN YOU MARRY? - CALIFORNIA MARRIAGE LAWS

Basic Authority: Marriage requirements are the jurisdiction of the individual states.

Up to 1880 there were no restrictions in California about who could marry whom.

1880 - Marriages between whites and "negro, mulatto, or Mongolians" were prohibited in California.

1933 - Malays were added to the list of those with whom whites could not marry in California. (This was to confirm that Filipinos could not marry whites in California.)

1948 - California Supreme Court declares anti-miscegenation laws in California to be unconstitutional.

1965 - U.S. Supreme Court declares anti-miscegenation laws unconsitutional anywhere in the United States.

Notes

Chapter 1: Chinese Predecessors

1. Ben Hoang, interview with author, 1982 and 1983; Mary Lee, interview with author, 1997; and Roderick Jone, interview with author, 1997.
2. Sandy Lydon, *Chinese Gold: The Chinese in the Monterey Bay Region* (Capitola, Calif.: Capitola Book Co., 1985), 119.
3. Lydon, *Chinese Gold*, 187.
4. Lydon, *Chinese Gold*, 134-135.
5. Viceroy T'ing-hsiang quoted in Thomas Chinn, ed., *A History of the Chinese in California: A Syllabus* (San Francisco: Chinese Historical Society, 1969, 12-13.
6. Lydon, *Chinese Gold*, 79-111.

Chapter 2: Japanese Background

1. Robert S. Ozaki, *The Japanese: A Cultural Portrait* (Rutland, Vt.: Tuttle, 1978), 35-36. Noel Perrin, *Giving Up the Gun: Japan's Reversion to the Sword, 1543-1879* (Boston: David R. Godine, 1979), 5-7. Perrin tells the remarkable story of how the Japanese eventually banned the use of guns in their warfare.
2. As quoted in Katherine Plummer, *The Shogun's Reluctant Ambassadors: Sea Drifters* (Tokyo: Lotus Press, 1984), 23.
3. John W. Connor, *Tradition and Change in Three Generations of Japanese Americans* (Chicago: Nelson-Hall, 1977), 9.
4. Takie Sugiyama Lebra, *Japanese Patterns of Behavior* (Honolulu: University Press of Hawaii, 1976), 79-109; John F. McDermott, Jr., Wen-Shing Tseng, and Thomas W. Maretzki, *People and Cultures of Hawaii: A Psychocultural Profile* (Honolulu: University Press of Hawaii, 1980), 84-90; Edison Uno, "Japanese

Behaviorial [sic] Characteristics, Values, and Cultural Personality Traits" (n.p., n.d., typescript), a 2-page summary of characteristics.
5. Peter Duus, *The Japanese Discovery of America: A Brief History with Documents* (Boston: Bedford Books, 1997).
6. Duus, *Japanese Discovery*, 155.
7. Masakiyo Yanagawa, "The First Japanese Mission to America," *Life* 12, no. 8 (23 February 1942): 84.
8. Duus, *Japanese Discovery*, 174.
9. *Watsonville Pajaronian*, 7 August 1873.
10. *Watsonville Pajaronian*, 8 March 1877; *Salinas Index*, 1 March 1877. The Salinas paper also did a summary of the event on 21 December 1934, though the date of that clipping is in dispute.
11. *Watsonville Pajaronian*, 28 November 1872.
12. *Santa Cruz Sentinel*, 31 October 1874.
13. Yuji Ichioka, *The Issei: The World of the First Generation Japanese Immigrants, 1885-1924* (New York: Free Press, 1988), 13-14.
14. David J. O'Brien and Stephen S. Fugita, *The Japanese American Experience* (Bloomington: Indiana University Press, 1991), 12.
15. Duus, *Japanese Discovery*, 1.

Chapter 3: First Beginning

1. *Santa Cruz Sentinel*, 10 March 1887; *Santa Cruz Sentinel*, 15 April 1887.
2. Kazuko Nakane, *Nothing Left in My Hands: An Early Japanese American Community in California's Pajaro Valley* (Seattle: Young Pine Press, 1985), 26-28.
3. *Watsonville Pajaronian*, 15 March 1900; *Watsonville Pajaronian*, 17 May 1900; Nakane, *Nothing Left*, 25-26.

4. *Watsonville Pajaronian*, 28 September 1893.

5. *Watsonville Pajaronian*, 26 December 1895.

6. *Watsonville Pajaronian*, 20 September 1900.

7. *Watsonville Pajaronian*, 22 November 1900.

8. Ichioka, *Issei*, 79-81.

9. Lydon, *Chinese Gold*, 105.

10. *Watsonville Pajaronian*, 20 July 1905.

11. Luke P. Cikuth, *The Pajaro Valley Apple Industry, 1890-1930*; oral history transcript of tape-recorded interview conducted by Elizabeth S. Calciano in 1964 (Regional History Project of the University Library, University of California, Santa Cruz, 1967), 124.

12. Ichioka, *Issei*, 82.

13. Porter Family ledger, 1901.

14. For a complete analysis of the move, see Lydon, *Chinese Gold*, 184-191

15. *Watsonville Pajaronian*, 29 April 1897.

16. "Yamato Cemetery History, 1908-1976" (Salinas), 2.

17. *Watsonville Pajaronian*, 30 April 1896.

18. *Watsonville Pajaronian*, 3 February 1902.

19. *Watsonville Pajaronian*, 12 April 1910; *Salinas Index*, 4 June 1910.

20. Karen Clare, "Early Pioneers of San Juan Bautista," *Monterey Herald Weekend Magazine*, 17 March 1985.

21. Lydon, *Chinese Gold*, 377-380.

22. Toshio Oba, *The History of the Fishing Industry Using Diving Equipment in Southern Chiba Prefecture* (title translated from Japanese), 1994; and A. L. "Scrap" Lundy, *The California Abalone Industry: A Pictorial History* (Flagstaff, Ariz.: Best Pub. Co., 1997).

23. *Santa Cruz Surf*, 26 January 1907.

24. *Watsonville Pajaronian*, 12 April 1900.

25. See Ichioka, *Issei*. There are three naturalized Issei in the region in the 1900 Census.

26. *Watsonville Pajaronian*, 18 May 1905.

27. Ichioka, *Issei*, 52-53.

28. *Santa Cruz Sentinel*, 11 February 1904; *Santa Cruz Sentinel*, 12 February 1904.

29. *Watsonville Pajaronian*, 12 January 1905.

30. Roger Daniels, *Politics of Prejudice: The Anti-Japanese Movement in California and the Struggle for Japanese Exclusion* (Berkeley: University of California Press, 1977), 24-25.

CHAPTER 4: ERA OF THE FIRST FAMILIES

1. Eliot G. Mears, *Resident Orientals on the American Pacific Coast: Their Legal and Economic Status* (Chicago: University of Chicago Press, 1928), Appendix, Document D, "The Gentleman's Agreement," 443.

2. Ichioka, *Issei*, 164-166.

3. Ozaki, *Japanese*, 281.

4. Nakane, *Nothing Left*, 56.

5. Santa Cruz County Sheriff's Office, "Santa Cruz County Arrest Records," Case #3984 (3 December 1918), 224, Special Collections, University Library, University of California, Santa Cruz. Kamigaka was 28 years old and a native of Japan.

6. *Watsonville Pajaronian*, 10 August 1912.

7. *Watsonville Pajaronian*, 23 April 1913.

8. *Santa Cruz Sentinel*, 26 October 1919.

9. Walter Beach, *Oriental Crime in California: A Study of Offenses Committed by Orientals in That State, 1900-1927* (Stanford: Stanford University Press, 1932).

10. "Yamato Cemetery History."

11. David T. Yamada and Oral History Committee, Monterey Peninsula Japanese American Citizens League, *The Japanese of the Monterey Peninsula: Their History & Legacy, 1895-1995* (Monterey, Calif.: Monterey Peninsula Japanese American Citizens League, 1995), 173-175.

12. *Santa Cruz Surf*, 3 November 1910.

13. Edwin O. Reischauer and Marius B. Jansen, *The Japanese Today: Change and Continuity*, enl. ed. (Cambridge, Mass.: Belknap Press of Harvard University Press, 1995), 212-214.

14. See Ichioka, *Issei*, 16-18, for a general discussion. Also note that he says that there is a Methodist mission in Watsonville in 1895.

15. Ichioka, *Issei*, 176.

16. *Watsonville Evening Pajaronian*, 29 December 1909 and 10 January 1910. See also Eleanor Johnson, *The Japanese and Japanese-Americans in the Pajaro Valley* (Watsonville, Calif.: Japanese American Citizens League, 1967), 14.

17. Kim Sakamoto, personal communication, June 1997.

18. *Santa Cruz Surf*, 5 March 1907.

19. *Monterey New Era*, 16 March 1904.

20. *Santa Cruz Surf*, 11 June 1907.

21. See Lydon, *Chinese Gold*, 288-289.

22. Agreement between Jacks Corporation and Onojiro Uchida, 8 January 1910, Box 10, David Jacks Collection, Huntington Library, San Marino, California.

23 For the lumber industry, see Michael Barbour, John Evarts, and Sandy Lydon, et al., *Coast Redwoods: A Cultural and Natural History* (Los Olivos, Calif.: Cachuma Press, forthcoming). For the Molino Timber Company, see Albretto Stoodley, "Loma Prieta Lumber Company" (n.p., n.d.), 45 leaves, Special Collections, University Library, University of California, Santa Cruz.

24. Tom Mangelsdorf, *A History of Steinbeck's Cannery Row* (Santa Cruz, Calif.: Western Tanager Press, 1986), 9.

25. *Monterey Cypress,* 28 March 1911.

26. *Monterey Cypress,* 28 July 1907; summary article from the *Cypress* was copied in the *Watsonville Evening Pajaronian,* 22 November 1910.

27. *Watsonville Evening Pajaronian,* 17 April 1917.

28. William L. Scofield, "*Sardine Fishing Methods at Monterey, California,*" Division of Fish and Game of California, Fish Bulletin no. 19 (Sacramento: California State Printing Office, 1929), 17.

29. *Monterey New Era,* 23 January 1908.

30. *Watsonville Pajaronian,* 19 January 1916.

31. *Monterey Cypress,* 1 June 1910.

32. Lease signed by David Jacks, O. Noda, and S. Nao, 1 November 1906, Box 16, David Jacks Collection.

33. *Monterey New Era,* 23 January 1908.

34. *Watsonville Pajaronian,* 7 December 1909.

35. *Monterey Cypress,* 9 November 1910. A preliminary survey of Santa Cruz County lease records shows a scattering of leases signed in 1910 and 1911, but in 1912, there are 28 leases registered involving Japanese farmers in Santa Cruz County. This startling spike in the statistics was caused, at least in part, by the discussion in Sacramento over a law to limit the length of leases signed by aliens ineligible for citizenship. (Further research in the Monterey and San Benito County lease books will be necessary before we can determine whether the patterns in Santa Cruz County were duplicated elsewhere.)

36. H. Brett Melendy, *The Oriental Americans* (New York: Hippocrene Books, 1972), 117ff.

37. *Salinas Index,* 27 September 1909.

38. *Watsonville Pajaronian,* 23 May 1913.

39. *Watsonville Pajaronian,* 11 June 1917, has the entire list of registrants by precinct. Also, the Salinas story comes from the *Watsonville Pajaronian,* 8 August 1917.

40. Japanese Agricultural Association, "The Japanese Farmers in California" (San Francisco: Japanese Agricultural Association, 1918), 28.

41. *Watsonville Pajaronian,* 27 June 1917.

42. Japanese Agricultural Association, "Japanese," 31.

43. *Watsonville Pajaronian,* 5 July 1917.

44. "The History of the Japanese Presbyterian Mission Hall of Salinas," typescript, n.p, n.d. Document in possession of author.

45. Santa Cruz County, Deed Books, 10: 189 (21 October 1924). Apparently, Taoka had registered his discharge with the county in order to establish the possibility of becoming a naturalized citizen.

46. *Watsonville Pajaronian,* 3 September 1918.

47. *Watsonville Pajaronian,* 5 July 1917.

48. *Watsonville Pajaronian,* 5 January 1918.

49. *Watsonville Pajaronian,* 5 January 1918; *Santa Cruz Surf,* 4 January 1918.

50. Daniels, *Politics of Prejudice,* 85.

51. *Watsonville Pajaronian,* 29 December 1919.

52. Ichioka, *Issei,* 227-237.

CHAPTER 5: NISEI GENERATION

1. Duncan Chin, *Growing Up On Grove Street, 1931-1946: Sketches and Memories of a Chinese-American Boyhood* (Capitola, Calif.: Capitola Book Co., 1995), xi.

2. Yamada, *Japanese,* 75.

3. Clare, "Early Pioneers of San Juan Bautista."

4. Santa Cruz County, Deed Books, 169: 119 (29 May 1927); 51: 457 (15 January 1925); 172: 450 (27 February 1926). See also, Mears, *Resident Orientals,* 352.

5. *Santa Cruz Sentinel,* 29 January, 1922.

6. Live Oak Parent-Teacher Improvement Club, Minutes, 20 January 1922.

7. "The Ku Klux Klan: Yesterday, Today and Forever," brochure published by the KKK, n.p., n.d., unpaginated.

8. *Twin Lakes Moon,* 26 April 1924.

9. Ichioka, *Issei,* 198-206.

10. Mears, *Resident Orientals,* 355.

11. See "Black History, Watsonville Style," in the *Watsonville Register-Pajaronian*, 18 February 1989.

12. Lydon, *Chinese Gold*, 169-174.

13. California Political Code, Art X, par. 1662, as quoted in Mears, *Resident Orientals*, 354.

14. Ronald T. Takaki, *Strangers from a Different Shore: A History of Asian Americans* (Boston: Little, Brown, 1989), 222-223.

15. Sandy Lydon, *A Half-Century of Service: The Watsonville Japanese American Citizens League, 1934-1984* (Watsonville, Calif.: JACL, 1984), 13.

16. Yamada, *Japanese*, 175-177.

17. Adon Poli, *Japanese Farm Holdings on the Pacific Coast* (Berkeley: U.S. Department of Agriculture, Bureau of Agricultural Economics, 1944), 15.

18. Cikuth, *Pajaro Valley Apple Industry*, 124.

19. Arne Kallan, "Sea Tenure and the Japanese Experience: Resource Management in Coastal Fisheries," in *Unwrapping Japan: Society and Culture in Anthropological Perspective*, ed. Eyal Ben-Ari, Brian Moeran, and James Valentine (Honolulu: University of Hawaii Press, 1990), 197.

20. Mears, *Resident Orientals*, 236.

21. *Monterey New Era*, 7 June 1899 and 28 June 1899.

22. *Monterey New Era*, 23 August 1899.

23. *Monterey Cypress*, 19 August 1899.

24. *Monterey New Era*, 23 August 1899.

25. *Monterey New Era*, 4 October 1899.

26. Paul Bonnot, "California Abalones," *California Fish and Game* 26, no. 3 (1940): 209.

27. W. W. Curtner, "Observations on the Growth and Habits of the Red and Black Abalone" (master's thesis, Stanford University, 1917), unpaginated.

28. Paul Bonnot, 1938, p. 204.

29. *Oakland Tribune*, 6 June 1937.

30. Oba, *History of the Fishing Industry, 161.*

31. Toshio Oba, personal communication, Tateyama, Japan, April 1996.

CHAPTER 6: WAR YEARS

1. Ichiro Yamaguchi, "*Nisei Christian Journey: Its Promise & Fulfillment,*" 1983, vol. 2, p. 80.

2. For further reading on the wartime internment, see U.S. Commission on Wartime Relocation and Internment of Civilians, *Personal Justice Denied* (Washington: Government Printing Office, 1982); Roger Daniels, *Concentration Camps, North America: Japanese in the United States and Canada During World War II* , rev. ed. (Malabar, Fla.: Krieger, 1981); Peter Irons, *Justice at War: The Story of the Japanese American Internment Cases* (New York: Oxford University Press, 1983); and Peter Irons, ed., *Justice Delayed: The Record of the Japanese American Internment Cases* (Middletown, Con.: Wesleyan University Press, 1989).

3. *Hollister Evening Free Lance*, 8 December 1941.

4. *Hollister Evening Free Lance*, 10 December 1941.

5. Bunyu Fujimura, *Though I Be Crushed: The Wartime Experiences of a Buddhist Minister* (Los Angeles: Nembutsu Press, 1985), 45.

6. Paul D. Johnston, *Aptos and the Mid-Santa Cruz County Area from the 1890s through World War II*, oral history transcript of tape-recorded interview conducted by Elizabeth S. Calciano in 1965 and 1966 (Regional History Project of the University Library, University of California, Santa Cruz, 1973), 187.

7. Miller Freeman, editoral, *Pacific Fisherman*, September 1942, p. 10.

8. Earl Warren, as quoted in Daniels, *Concentration Camps,* 76.

9. As quoted in *Santa Cruz Sentinel*, 2 February 1942.

10. *Santa Cruz Sentinel*, 4 February 1942.

11. *Santa Cruz Sentinel*, 2 February 1942.

12 See Geoffrey Dunn, "Male Notte: Santa Cruz-Italian Relocation and Restrictions during World War II," *Santa Cruz County History Journal 1* (1994): 82-89.

13. DeWitt quoted in *New York Times*, 4 March 1942, p. 1.

14. Sandy Lydon, *Fifty Years of Continuous Service to Community; The San Benito County Japanese American Citizens League: A Short History* (San Juan Bautista: Japanese American Citizens League, 1985), 30.

15. *Santa Cruz Sentinel News*, 8 April 1942.

16. April Arao, from an interview of her parents, May 1984.

17. San Benito County Board of Supervisors, Minutes 12 (1 April 1943), 172.

18. Roger Daniels, *Prisoners without Trial: Japanese Americans in World War II (New York: Hill and Wang, 1993),* 64.

19. Felicia Mai Hashimoto, "A Close Examination of the Japanese Agriculture Community in Watsonville,

California," unpublished paper, 13 pages, for Anthropology 181, UCSC, March 19, 1996.

20. Poli, Japanese Farm Holdings, 12.

21. Poli, Japanese Farm Holdings, 26ff.

22. Poli, Japanese Farm Holdings.

23. Melendy, *Oriental Americans,*163, cites California Statutes: 1943: 1059, 10000 and California Statutes 1945: 181, 1129.

24. See Melendy, *Oriental Americans*, 166. He also cites Audrie Girdner and Anne Loftis, *The Great Betrayal: The Evacuation of the Japanese-Americans During World War II* (New York: Macmillan, 1969), 432. Also see *Monterey Cypress*, 8 June 1948.

25. See *Monterey Peninsula Herald*, 14 May 1949.

Chapter 7: Second Beginning

1. Salinas Chamber of Commerce, "Survey of Attitudes of Salinas Citizens Toward Japanese-Americans During World War II" (n.d., typescript copy), Special Collections, Salinas Public Library.

2. Ibid., 8.

3. *Hollister Evening Free Lance*, 27 September 1945.

4. Ibid.

5. *Hollister Evening Free Lance*, 19 December 1945.

6. Chamber of Commerce and Agriculture of the Pajaro Valley, *Newsletter*, 17 September 1945.

7. Kay Izumizaki, interview, December 1995.

8. *Monterey Peninsula Herald*, 11 May 1945.

9. Yamada, *Japanese*, 93-96.

10. Bill Ong Hing, *Making and Remaking Asian America Through Immigration Policy, 1850-1990* (Stanford: Stanford University Press, 1993), 56. For details on the McCarran-Walter Act, see Frank L. Auerbach, *Immigration Laws of the United States*, 2d ed. (Indianapolis: Bobbs-Merrill, 1961), 16-17.

11. Auerbach, *Immigration Laws*, 19-20.

12. Harry Fukutome, interview with author, 1980.

13. Hing, *Making and Remaking*, 106.

14. Hashimoto, *"A Close Examination,"* 8.

15. *Wall Street Journal*, 8 August 1972.

16. *Asahi Evening News* (Tokyo), 29 July 1974, p. 1.

17. *San Francisco Chronicle*, 5 May 1973.

18. Roger Daniels, *Asian America: Chinese and Japanese in the United States Since 1850* (Seattle: University of Washington Press, 1988), 341-342. Alethea Yip,

"Remembering Vincent Chin," *Asian Week 18*, no. 43 (13 June 1997):12-13.

19. See Harry H. L. Kitano, *Generations and Identity: The Japanese American* (Needham Heights, Mass.: Ginn Press, 1993), 126-127.

BIBLIOGRAPHY

Arao, April. Interview of parents. May 1984.

Asahi Evening News. Newspaper. Published in Tokyo.

Auerbach, Frank L. *Immigration Laws of the United States.* 2d ed. Indianapolis: Bobbs-Merrill, 1961.

Barbour, Michael, John Evarts, and Sandy Lydon, et al. *Coast Redwoods: A Cultural and Natural History.* Los Olivos, Calif.: Cachuma Press, forthcoming.

Beach, Walter. *Oriental Crime in California: A Study of Offenses Committed by Orientals in That State, 1900-1927.* Stanford: Stanford University Press, 1932.

Bonnot, Paul. "California Abalones." *California Fish and Game* 26, no. 3 (1940): 209.

California Political Code. Art X, par. 1662. Quoted in Eliot G. Mears, *Resident Orientals on the American Pacific Coast: Their Legal and Economic Status* (Chicago: University of Chicago Press, 1928), 354.

California Statutes. 1943: 1059, 10000. Quoted in H. Brett Melendy, *The Oriental Americans* (New York: Hippocrene Books, 1972), 163.

California Statutes. 1945: 181, 1129. Quoted in H. Brett Melendy, *The Oriental Americans* (New York: Hippocrene Books, 1972), 163.

Chamber of Commerce and Agriculture of the Pajaro Valley. *Newsletter,* 17 September 1945.

Chin, Duncan. *Growing Up On Grove Street, 1931-1946: Sketches and Memories of a Chinese-American Boyhood.* Capitola, Calif.: Capitola Book Co., 1995.

Chin, Thomas, ed. *A History of the Chinese in California: A Syllabus.* San Francisco: Chinese Historical Society, 1969.

Cikuth, Luke P. *The Pajaro Valley Apple Industry, 1890-1930.* Oral history transcript of tape-recorded interview conducted by Elizabeth S. Calciano in 1964. Regional History Project of the University Library, University of California, Santa Cruz, 1967.

Clare, Karen. "Early Pioneers of San Juan Bautista." *Monterey Herald Weekend Magazine,* 17 March 1985.

Connor, John W. *Tradition and Change in Three Generations of Japanese Americans.* Chicago: Nelson-Hall, 1977.

Curtner, W. W. "Observations on the Growth and Habits of the Red and Black Abalone." Master's thesis, Stanford University, 1917.

Daniels, Roger. *Asian America: Chinese and Japanese in the United States Since 1850.* Seattle: University of Washington Press, 1988.

_____. *Concentration Camps, North America: Japanese in the United States and Canada During World War II.* Rev. ed. Malabar, Fla.: Krieger, 1981.

_____. *Politics of Prejudice: The Anti-Japanese Movement in California and the Struggle for Japanese Exclusion.* Berkeley: University of California Press, 1977.

_____. *Prisoners without Trial: Japanese Americans in World War II.* New York: Hill and Wang, 1993.

Dunn, Geoffrey. "Male Notte: Santa Cruz-Italian Relocation and Restrictions during World War II." *Santa Cruz County History Journal* 1 (1994): 82-89.

Duus, Peter. *The Japanese Discovery of America: A Brief History with Documents.* Boston: Bedford Books, 1997.

Freeman, Miller. Editorial. *Pacific Fisherman,* September 1942, 10.

Fujimura, Bunyu. *Though I Be Crushed: The Wartime Experiences of a Buddhist Minister.* Los Angeles: Nembutsu Press, 1985.

Fukutome, Harry. Interview with author, 1980.

Girdner, Audrie, and Anne Loftis. *The Great Betrayal: The Evacuation of the Japanese-Americans During World War II.* New York: Macmillan, 1969.

Hashimoto, Felicia Mai. "A Close Examination of the Japanese Agricultural Community in Watsonville, California." March 1996.

Hing, Bill Ong. *Making and Remaking Asian America Through Immigration Policy, 1850-1990.* Stanford: Stanford University Press, 1993.

"The History of the Japanese Presbyterian Mission Hall of Salinas." N.p, n.d.   Typescript.   Author's collection.

Hoang, Ben. Interview with author. 1982 and 1983.

Hollister Evening Free Lance. Newspaper. Published in Hollister, California.

Ichioka, Yuji. *The Issei: The World of the First Generation Japanese Immigrants, 1885-1924.* New York: Free Press, 1988.

Irons, Peter. *Justice at War: The Story of the Japanese American Internment Cases.* New York: Oxford University Press, 1983.

_____, ed. *Justice Delayed: The Record of the Japanese American Internment Cases.* Middletown, Con.: Wesleyan University Press, 1989.

Izumizaki, Kay. Interview with author. December 1995..

[Jacks Collection]. David Jacks Collection, Huntington Library, San Marino, California

Japanese Agricultural Association. "The Japanese Farmers in California." Japanese Agricultural Association, San Francisco, 1918.

Johnson, Eleanor. *The Japanese and Japanese-Americans in the Pajaro Valley.* Watsonville, Calif.: Japanese American Citizens League, 1967.

Johnston, Paul D. *Aptos and the Mid-Santa Cruz County Area from the 1890s through World War II.* Oral history transcript of tape-recorded interview conducted by Elizabeth S. Calciano in 1965 and 1966. Regional History Project of the University Library, University of California, Santa Cruz, 1973.

Jone, Roderick. Interview with author. 1997.

Kallan, Arne. "Sea Tenure and the Japanese Experience: Resource Management in Coastal Fisheries." In *Unwrapping Japan: Society and Culture in Anthropological Perspective,* edited by Eyal Ben-Ari, Brian Moeran, and James Valentine. Honolulu: University of Hawaii Press, 1990.

Kitano, Harry H. L. *Generations and Identity: The Japanese American.* Needham Heights, Mass.: Ginn Press, 1993.

Ku Klux Klan. "The Ku Klux Klan: Yesterday, Today and Forever." KKK. N.p., n.d.   Unpaginated brochure.

Lebra, Takie Sugiyama. *Japanese Patterns of Behavior.* Honolulu: University Press of Hawaii, 1976.

Lee, Mary. Interview with author. 1997.

Live Oak Parent-Teacher and Improvement Club. Minutes, 20 January 1922.

Lundy, A.L. "Scrap". *The California Abalone Industry: A Pictorial History.* Flagstaff, Ariz.: Best Pub. C., 1997.

Lydon, Sandy. *Chinese Gold: The Chinese in the Monterey Bay Region.* Capitola, Calif.: Capitola Book Co., 1985.

_____.. *Fifty Years of Continuous Service to Community; The San Benito County Japanese American Citizens League: A Short History.* San Juan Bautista, Calif.: JACL, 1985.

_____. *A Half-Century of Service: The Watsonville Japanese American Citizens League, 1934-1984.* Watsonville, Calif.: JACL, 1984.

Mangelsdorf, Tom. *A History of Steinbeck's Cannery Row.* Santa Cruz, Calif.: Western Tanager Press, 1986.

McDermott, John F., Jr., Wen-Shing Tseng, and Thomas W. Maretzki. *People and Cultures of Hawaii: A Psychocultural Profile.* Honolulu: University Press of Hawaii, 1980.

Mears, Eliot G. *Resident Orientals on the American Pacific Coast: Their Legal and Economic Status.* Chicago: University of Chicago Press, 1928.

Melendy, H. Brett. *The Oriental Americans.* New York: Hippocrene Books, 1972.

Monterey Cypress. Newspaper. Published in Monterey, California.

Monterey New Era. Newspaper. Published in Monterey, California.

Monterey Peninsula Herald. Newspaper. Published in Monterey, California.

Nakane, Kazuko. *Nothing Left in My Hands: An Early Japanese American Community in California's Pajaro Valley.* Seattle: Young Pine Press, 1985.

Oakland Tribune. Newspaper. Published in Oakland, California.

Oba, Toshio. *The History of the Fishing Industry Using Diving Equipment in Southern Chiba Prefecture.* 1994.

Oba, Toshio. Personal communication. April 1996.

O'Brien, David J., and Stephen S. Fugita. *The Japanese American Experience.* Bloomington: Indiana University Press, 1991.

Ozaki, Robert S. *The Japanese: A Cultural Portrait.* Rutland, Vt.: Tuttle, 1978.

Perrin, Noel. *Giving Up the Gun: Japan's Reversion to the Sword, 1543-1879.* Boston: David R. Godine, 1979.

Plummer, Katherine. *The Shogun's Reluctant Ambassadors: Sea Drifters.* Tokyo: Lotus Press, 1984.

Poli, Adon. *Japanese Farm Holdings on the Pacific Coast.* Berkeley: U.S. Department of Agriculture, Bureau of Agricultural Economics, 1944.

Porter Family ledger, 1901.

Reischauer, Edwin O., and Marius B. Jansen. *The Japanese Today: Change and Continuity.* Enl. ed. Cambridge, Mass. : Belknap Press of Harvard University Press, 1995.

Sakamoto, Kim. Personal communication. June 1997.

Salinas Chamber of Commerce. "Survey of Attitudes of Salinas Citizens Toward Japanese-Americans During World War II." N.d. Typescript copy. Special Collections, Salinas Public Library.

Salinas Index. Newspaper. Published in Salinas, California.

San Benito County Board of Supervisors. Minutes. County Courthouse, Hollister, California.

San Francisco Chronicle. Newspaper. Published in San Francisco, California.

Santa Cruz County. Deed Books. County Recorder's Office, Santa Cruz, California.

Santa Cruz County Sheriff's Office."Santa Cruz County Arrest Records." Special Collections, University Library, University of California, Santa Cruz.

Santa Cruz Sentinel. Newspaper. Published in Santa Cruz, California.

Santa Cruz Surf. Newspaper. Published in Santa Cruz, California.

Scofield, William L. "Sardine Fishing Methods at Monterey, California." Division of Fish and Game of California, Fish Bulletin no. 19. Sacramento: California State Printing Office, 1929.

Stoodley, Albretto. "Loma Prieta Lumber Company." Special Collections, University Library, University of California, Santa Cruz.

Takaki, Ronald T. *Strangers from a Different Shore: A History of Asian Americans.* Boston: Little, Brown, 1989.

Twin Lakes Moon, 26 April 1924.

U.S. Commission on Wartime Relocation and Internment of Civilians. *Personal Justice Denied.* Washington: Government Printing Office, 1982.

Uno, Edison. "Japanese Behaviorial [sic] Characteristics, Values, and Cultural Personality Traits." Np., n.d. Typescript.

Wall Street Journal. Newspaper.

Watsonville Pajaronian. Newspaper. Published in Watsonville, California.

Yamada, David T., and Oral History Committee, Monterey Peninsula Japanese American Citizens League. *The Japanese of the Monterey Peninsula: Their History & Legacy, 1895-1995.* Monterey, Calif.: Monterey Peninsula Japanese American Citizens League, 1995.

Yamaguchi, Ichiro. "Nisei Christian Journey: Its Promise & Fulfillment." 1983, vol. 2:80.

"Yamato Cemetery History, 1908-1976." Salinas.

Yanagawa, Masakiyo. "The First Japanese Mission to America." *Life* 12, no. 8 (23 February 1942): 84.

Yip, Alethea. "Remembering Vincent Chin." *Asian Week* 18, no. 43 (13 June 1997):12-13.

Index

Page numbers for illustrations are in italics.

OTHER QUALITY TITLES FROM CAPITOLA BOOK COMPANY

- Duncan Chin. *Growing Up On Grove Street: Sketches of a Chinese-American Boyhood.* A collection of memories and sketches providing an insight into a childhood in a multi-cultural neighborhood in Watsonville. Paperback with extensive sketches and photographs.

- Geoffrey Dunn. *Santa Cruz Is In the Heart.* A series of sensitive and thoughtful essays by a Santa Cruz native son. Paperback with photographs.

- Sandy Lydon. *Chinese Gold: The Chinese in the Monterey Bay Region.* An award-winning book which tells the story of the Chinese in the Monterey Bay Region. Paparback with hundreds of poignant and informative photographs.

- Morton Marcus. *Santa Cruz Mountain Poems.* A collection of brilliant poems written by one the region's most revered and beloved poets. Paperback lavishly illustrated by Gary H. Brown.

Have your bookstore order them, or place an order directly:

Capitola Book Company
1601 41st Avenue, Suite 202
Capitola, CA 95010

Designer	Chris Lydon, Aptos, California
Text	12/14 Garamond
Display	Garamond
Printer	Malloy Lithographing, Ann Arbor, Michigan
Binder	Malloy Lithographing, Ann Arbor, Michigan